Tony Harrison

TONY HARRISON

Moira Conway

Tony Harrison

Joe Kelleher

Northcote House

in association with
The British Council

First published in 1996 by Northcote House Publishers Ltd, Plymbridge House, Estover Road, Plymouth PL6 7PY, United Kingdom. Tel: +44 (0) 1752 202368. Fax: +44 (0) 1752 202330.

British Library Cataloguing-in-Publication Data
A catalogue record for this book is available from the British Library

ISBN 0 7463 0789 6

Typeset by PDQ Typesetting, Newcastle-under-Lyme
Printed and bound in the United Kingdom

Contents

Biographical Outline

1937   Harrison born 30 April in Beeston area, Leeds.
1948   Wins scholarship to Leeds Grammar School.
1958   Graduates with BA in Classics from Leeds University.
          Begins PhD which is not completed.
1962–6   Lectures at Ahmadu Bello University, Nigeria.
1964   *Earthworks* by T. W. Harrison.
1966   *Aikin Mata* published, co-written with James Simmons,
          and first performed at Ahmadu Bello in 1964.
1966–7   Teaches at Charles University, Prague.
1967–9   Northern Arts Literary Fellowship at Universities of
          Newcastle and Durham. The poem-pamphlet *Newcastle is
          Peru* published (1969).
1969   UNESCO Fellowship and travel in Cuba, Brazil, Senegal
          and Gambia.
1970   *The Loiners*, Harrison's first full-length book of poetry,
          published.
1973   *The Misanthrope* his version of Molière, performed by the
          National Theatre at the Old Vic, and published.
1973–4   Gregynog Arts Fellowship at the University of Wales.
1975   *Phaedra Britannica* performed and published; composes
          lyrics for George Cukor's film of Maeterlinck's *The Blue
          Bird*; and *Palladas: Poems* published.
1976–7   Second Northern Arts Literary Fellowship.
1977   *Bow Down* performed by the National Theatre at the
          Cottesloe and published; Harrison working as the
          National Theatre's resident dramatist and *The Passion*
          (later part of *The Mysteries*) published.
1978   His version of Sabina's Czech libretto for Smetana's opera
          The Bartered Bride commissioned by the New York

Metropolitan Opera, performed and published; *From 'The School of Eloquence' and Other Poems* published.

1979–80 UK/US Bicentennial Fellowship at New York Metropolitan Opera House.

1980 Wins the national Poetry Competition for 'Timer'.

1981 *Continuous: 50 Sonnets from 'The School of Eloquence'*, an expansion of the sequence, published; *Arctic Paradise*, with Harrison's verse commentary, broadcast; his version of *The Oresteia* performed by the National Theatre and published; pamphlet, *A Kumquat for John Keats* and translations *U. S. Martial* published.

1983 *Yan Tan Tethera*, a collaboration with Harrison Birtwistle commissioned by the BBC, performed in London. Wins the first European Poetry Translation Prize for *The Oresteia*.

1984 *The Big H* a music drama for children, produced in collaboration with Andree Molyneux and Dominic Muldowney, broadcast on BBC television; the first edition of *Selected Poems* published.

1985 *The Mysteries* performed at the National Theatre and broadcast by Channel 4; *Medea: a sex-war opera* commissioned by New York Metropolitan Opera but not performed; his long poem *v.*, written during the 1984 Miners' Strike, and *The Fire-Gap* published.

1986 *Theatre Works 1973–1985* published.

1987 The film/poems *Loving Memory*, directed by Peter Symes, broadcast; the second edition of *Selected Poems* published.

1987–8 President of the Classical Association.

1988 *The Trackers of Oxyrhyncus*, Harrison's play that develops the Sophoclean fragment *Ichneutae*, first performed at Delphi.

1989 *v. : new edition, with press articles* published, documenting the controversy over Richard Eyre's film of Harrison's reading of the poem, broadcast in 1987; the film/poem *The Blasphemers' Banquet*, Harrison's response to the Salman Rushdie affair, broadcast by BBC.

1990 Revised version of *The Trackers of Oxyrhyncus* performed at the National Theatre.

1991 The two-poem pamphlet *A Cold Coming: Gulf War Poems* published.

1992   His unperformed play *The Common Chorus* adapted from
        Aristophanes, published; the film/poem, *The Gaze of the
        Gorgon* broadcast; the full-length theatre piece *Square
        Rounds*, dealing with issues of twentieth-century
        militarism, directed by Harrison at the National Theatre;
        his volume of poems *The Gaze of the Gorgon* published.

1993   The film/poem *Black Daisies for the Bride*, set amongst
        Alzheimer's sufferers, broadcast by BBC and published;
        the unpublished play *Poetry or Bust* written for and
        performed at Salt's Mill in Bradford.

1994   The film/poem *A Maybe Day in Kazakhstan*, in part a
        response to the break-up of the former Soviet Union,
        broadcast by Channel 4.

1995   Harrison's play *The Kaisers of Carnuntum*, dealing with
        issues of cultural memory and historical violence, devised
        for and performed at the Roman amphitheatre at
        Carnuntum outside Vienna; his film/poem addressing
        the VJ commemorations *The Shadow of Hiroshima and other
        Film/Poems* and *Permanently Bard, Selected Poems of Tony
        Harrison* published. *The Guardian* newspaper publishes
        reports in verse by Harrison from the war in former
        Yugoslavia.

1996   *The Prince's Play*, Harrison's verse translation of Victor
        Hugo's *Le Roi S'Amuse* produced at the National Theatre.

Abbreviations and References

Astley   Neil Astley (ed.), *Tony Harrison: Bloodaxe Critical Anthologies 1* (Newcastle upon Tyne: Bloodaxe, 1991).

BD   *Black Daises for the Bride* (London: Faber, 1993).

CC   *The Common Chorus* (London: Faber, 1992).

EW   *Earthworks* (Leeds: Northern House, 1964).

GG   *The Gaze of the Gorgon* (Newcastle upon Tyne: Bloodaxe, 1992).

L   *The Loiners* (London Magazine Editions, 1970).

SH   *The Shadow of Hiroshima and other film/poems* (London: Faber, 1995).

SP   *Selected Poems*, 2nd edition (Harmondsworth: Penguin, 1987).

Spencer   Luke Spencer, *The Poetry of Tony Harrison* (Hemel Hempstead: Harvester Wheatsheaf, 1994).

TO   *The Trackers of Oxyrhyncus* (London: Faber, 1990).

TW   *Theatre Works 1973–1985* (Harmondsworth: Penguin, 1986).

Acknowledgements

The author and the publishers are grateful to Tony Harrison, Bloodaxe, Faber and Faber, and Penguin for permission to quote from the works of Tony Harrison.

Preface

Sometime in the late 1970s I discovered that a poet, a 'real poet', had attended Leeds Grammar School, the same school I was studying at, and had written real books. I took one of these, *The Loiners*, out of the public library at the first opportunity. I enjoyed, I think, at first, its clarity and certainty and I have been following this poet's work, off and on, ever since. Throughout, though, I have felt an uneasiness with the poetry's very eloquence, with its facility of speaking to me so clearly. For a start, although we were both LGS scholarship boys, Harrison's story was not my story. His was another time, for one thing, and the working-class homes of Beeston Hill were another scene from the grander homes of Gledhow that I grew up amongst. During certain sad, angry months of 1981 when people in this country turned to violence as a means of claiming something back, for their own, from a social structure that appeared to be shafting them, and rioting broke out in English inner cities, the Leeds version of all this stopped almost exactly at the bottom of our road. That seemed then to describe one of the unbreachable borders I was living on but could barely understand, and I still feel rather proud of this other Leeds boy who had crossed borders with impunity, and who managed to make it rhyme at the same time. This present piece is an attempt to engage at last, or for the first time, with my own parochial attachment to (my affection for) Harrison's work; but also with my own *uncertainty* (my fascination) with regard to that same clarity and impunity of Harrison's: that deliberation with which he throws himself into the breaches that have appeared against him. If I appear to be wanting it both ways here, I hope there is something in my position which chimes, humbly, with the tone of exemplary intellectual scepticism and rigorous self-questioning that runs throughout Harrison's own work.

In a book this short there are inevitably omissions. Rather than give a brief paragraph to every one of Harrison's writings, I have focused on certain works, but even then too briefly, at the expense of others. None of which is to imply in the slightest that the pieces not mentioned are not worth the reader's time. I hope, rather, that my comments make Harrison's works sound interesting enough to encourage the poetry-lover new to this poet to read as much as they can. Harrison's writing (his prose as well as his poetry) is deliberately pleasurable. His metres and rhymes are scores for a vocal musicality, and his arguments and polemics are always playful: playing the sensuality of verse and performance off against a structuring intelligence that is unable to resist jokes, provocations, puzzles, analogies. Harrison's work, like the clog-dancing satyrs in *Trackers* dances around borders, and we would want to dance with it.

The second level of omission concerns secondary critical material. I have avoided, again for want of space, giving an overview of Harrison's critical reception. I feel partly justified in this decision by the fact that, at present much of the most valuable of this material is collected in the excellent Bloodaxe anthology edited by Neil Astley (see Bibliography). I have largely restricted my borrowings from that volume to Harrison's own comments on his work, but the whole of that book is unreservedly recommended to the student of Harrison. The one exception to this general exclusion is Luke Spencer's *The Poetry of Tony Harrison*, the first book-length study of the poet. Spencer's work is also recommended by the present writer, and I have made acknowledgement here and there in my own text of certain moments when Spencer's intelligent readings and scholarship offer insights beyond what I can engage with here.

The third level of omission is any discussion of where Harrison himself is coming from in terms of literary and intellectual tradition. A full account would have to mention the ground-breaking work of cultural and social historians such as E. P. Thompson, Raymond Williams and Richard Hoggart; it would need to discuss issues of Classical Greek and Latin scholarship; it would need to speak of figures in the English literary 'canon' such as Milton, Keats, D. H. Lawrence; it would need to speak of opera; of 'modern poetry'; and it would need to reference also certain touchstones of vernacular and popular culture as are echoed throughout Harrison's work. Harrison's influences and interests are compendious, and although I hope I give the merest flavour of some of them, I have restricted my incorporation of 'extraneous' materials to texts that are *not* in fact part of the Harrisonian scene. Readers will notice, for example, various references to the Irish poet-dramatist W. B. Yeats. The intention here is to avoid drawing a list of 'influences' into the teleology of a Harrisonian *monument*, and draw Harrison's own work instead into a discussion, hints towards a discussion, of the conditions for a performative poetry (a poetry that may be one of theatre's saving graces) in general. This discussion would never simply concern itself with the technologies of rhyming and metrical rhythm (although it would include these things), but it *would* be concerned with the more sounding rhythms of historical remembering, political injunction, the mourning for and sceptical celebration of inheritance, and the staging of the personal upon the landscapes of 'our' lives. These are rhythms that speak over and against borders, these are ethical rhythms, and Harrison has done as much as anyone in the literary scene can do to make these rhythms heard.

1

Landscape, Lexicon and Love

Tony Harrison's *Selected Poems*, in its ordering of poems into
thematic groups irrespective of the precise order of their
publication, and in the erasure of the titles of particular
volumes, seems to offer itself as a version of the poet's complete
lyrical *oeuvre*, rather than as an interim 'selection' that refers to a
larger and more proper corpus.[1] Further, in its undisguised
autobiographical aspect (the book's heart is the ever-expanding
'from *The School of Eloquence*', documents of a life still being lived,
though the book already concludes with the poet's own epitaph)
Selected Poems invites one to approach it in terms appropriate to
the title of this series 'Writers and their Work' as something of a
Bildungsroman. If, in this context, we can take a narrative from the
book as a whole, we might describe a prominent aspect of that
narrative as a growing into, or laying claim to, a sexual maturity.
In this story that maturity is heterosexual and monogamous (more
on those terms later), but it is also a story of moving away from
home, of making a home of one's own, of measuring the ways one
returns to the places that have formed one, and taking the
measure of the changing self that makes those returns. With
regard to these latter aspects, which I shall again expand upon in
due course, the issue of maturity is staged by Harrison as a
political issue. In short, the politics one stages as one's own are
inextricably involved with one's ability to claim the maturity to
articulate and live those politics' implications. In short again –
although this time the statement is sufficient to sum up the case *in
toto* – in the earliest poems, first collected in *The Loiners* (1970, that
mucky book that Harrison's mother would apparently have
thrown upon the fire if it was not a library copy), political
perspicacity and the sentimental education of sex are, to all intents
and purposes, synonymous.

Basically, these early poems scratch at a sexual itch. They are largely dramatic poems, with named protagonists, but the poet's own persona seems to insinuate itself all the same into the protagonists' imaginative and lexical limitations. 'Ginger's Friday' is a fine example. The boy's experience of the voyeuristic primal scene of sexual knowledge – peeking in on Mrs Daley being straddled by her husband – is an initiation into desire and repression, the thrill of the scene and the fear of the punishment. Ginger's understandings of these things are not quite articulable, but are given sympathetic voice in the poet's own sardonic nostalgia over penances, perfumes, and pain:

> And no Hail Marys saved him from that Hell
> Where Daley's and his father's broad, black belts
> Cracked in the kitchen, and, blubbering, he smelt
> That burning rubber and burnt bacon smell.

(SP 15)

In these earliest poems, if the sexual itch finds a sublimation, it finds it in a poetic form of closed rhymes and too familiar images (too hauntingly familiar to the speaker) that return the itch to the protagonist as frustration, as a desublimated return of the itch itself. This apparently limitless process is Harrison's first theme, and like food for sexual fantasy one finds it, if one is looking for it, everywhere. 'The -*nuts* bit really -*nis*', as the curtailed opening sentence of 'The Pocket Wars of Peanuts Joe' has it, an *entendre* that is now uninhibitedly rendered in the present retelling of the story of Joe the self-exposer, the ejaculating pariah. The scene is of 'VD Day' (*sic*) celebrations, but Joe was no veteran, he lived his war 'window-gazing in the Surplus Stores', his only night-manoeuvres the ambushing of lovers in the public park as his own

> ack-ack ejac-
> *ulatio* shot through the dark
> Strewn, churned up trenches in his head.

Joe's onanism is imaginatively channelled by the poet into the myths then being played out around him in the VE celebrations ('It was something solemn made Joe flash/ His mitred bishop as they played *The King*'), but Joe is not thanked for his contribution by the celebrating populace and is carted off to prison, suicide, and a pathetic (if not comic) bequeathal of his gonads to the Pentagon: a displacement of 'Victory in Europe' (VE) to war-

2

efforts to come, in other places.

Joe's story is emblematic of Harrison's poetic at this time. The text is dense with particular details of home fondly and humorously recalled; but the poet who articulates the recollection makes a careful, and still distanced, reconciliation with the pariah to this scene – the outsider who is crazy, or unknowing enough, to make public the sexual itch that informs all recollections of the home scene, but which the scene itself brutally represses. The poet's reconciliation with this outsider sustains an ambiguity. He situates his own voice in the 'we' of those who knew they knew all there was to know about Joe; it is his own poeticisms that elaborate the fantastic ejaculations for which Joe is eventually punished; and it is his own act of recollection in this poem that makes a poetry of the social scene (and thereby to some extent a liberation from this scene of repressions) out of a desiring itch that, as far as the story goes, remains frustrated and bitterly lonely. Harrison's confident iambics, and the deliberation of his rhymes, while they don't so much frame the protagonist as prepare on his behalf an image-house in which his fantastic legend can take shape, still seem to be leaps ahead in knowingness – both of Joe and of the 'we' and 'they' staged throughout the poem. But the versification keeps Joe's danger (whatever that danger was) closed within the repressions of a nostalgia, which is as much a nostalgia for those repressive (and oppressive) social scenes as it is for their unassimilable sexual supplement

This poetic of a nostalgia, or an inheritance, that meditates on a once-forbidden sexuality in playful but crystalline rhymed iambics (more or less), reifies into a *dialect* as the verses accumulate. 'Allotments' takes the reader – and the poet – back again, to dad's plot and the scenery of first sexual encounters, where the young fumblers find their backsides already printed with the landscape's lexicon:

> The graveyards of Leeds 2
> Were hardly love-nests but they had to do [...]
> And after love we'd find some epitaph
> Embossed backwards on your arse and laugh.

> (*SP* 18)

These embossments, and others, remain imprinted, if not on the bum then at least in the mind's eye – the poet's own recall is testimony enough to this – and that imprint serves him now as something like a dialect in which to recall these scenes and events with fondness and fidelity (or as good as).[2] This dialect, however, to the extent that its imprint is indelible, is also a mechanism whereby those primary sexual explorations now appear to have been already consumed, penned in, by the historical circumstances of their occurrence. They are stuck there. The old Pole, 'that gabbling, foreign nut' who caught the kids 'at it', and who gives them a brief lecture on how the local abattoir chimneys that dominate the scene pun (for him) on those other chimneys at Auschwitz and Buchenwald, spikes the young man's dreams with a new and harsh knowledge:

> I smelt
> Lust on myself, then smoke, and then I felt
> Street bonfires blazing for the end of war
> V.E. and J. burn us like lights, but saw
> Lush prairies for a tumble, wide corrals,
> A Loiner's Elysium, and I cried
> For the family still pent up in my balls,
> For my corned beef sandwich, and for genocide.

This knowledge, like all the other knowledges pressed upon him by the scene, has become constitutive of the dialect in which the scenes of sexual longing can be recalled; and it is the procreative aspect of sex which seems most determinedly damned by that dialect as the verse – as if with an inevitability of its own motored by the rhyme scheme – channels the youngster's fantasies into terror. The wet dream is frustrated, or at best imaginatively sublimated into a lament for others, others long gone or yet to spring as damned as oneself from one's own balls; and if the proper sublimation of this tension is an adult poetry (Harrison's poetry), this is a poetry that cannot explode that tension so much as repeat its tumble around the mind's corral.

So much for hearth and home. In 1962, after not quite completing his second university degree, Harrison left England with his young family to teach in Nigeria.[3] The poem-sequence *The White Queen* is, one would assume, hardly autobiographical, but like the Leeds poems it does develop a dialect in which to address, if not a sexual politics of Harrison's own, a politicized understanding

4

compromised by the play of sexual desire in this particular landscape. The sequence, which plays out the tension between apparently illicit sexual desire and the lexical landscape which sublimates that desire into fantastic images of its own frustration and repression, is set in a neocolonial African ex-pat hell of booze, boredom, loathing and delirium:

> Where in one of many cold, white cells
> They play cold water on my testicles,
> When I should be breaking out...must...must
> Matchet the creeper from my strangled lust.

('Satyrae', *SP* 24)

Those narratives of othering and exclusion implied in the Leeds-based lyrics of *The Loiners* collection, themes of the sometimes fearful collective ranged against the solitary perpetrators of that collective's repressed sexual supplement, are writ large now in these scenarios of the encounter between Europeans and the fact of 'Africa'. Within these scenarios, with all the inheritance of European colonialism in Africa to inform the positioning of the protagonists (and their desire) and the poet's own metrical and lexical options, the powerplay of *The Loiners'* dialectical exploration of desire, repression, recollection and poetics is given a delirious twist.

Perhaps because of the difficulty of a European–African dialogue in these scenarios, the sexual instinct in these poems finds even more resistant forms of frustration. Or rather, within the particular economy of desire staged here, it is a frustration that resists even as it appears to invite. Africa and its bodies offer the European imagination fantastic forms for the poetic realization of libidinality, but, as in the quatrain quoted above, lust itself, and the desire to find satisfaction and liberation for it, though they both press into the rhyme words at the lines' endings, find company there with the 'cells' and 'testicles' that corral that desire within limit, prevention. Even as the enormity and, for the European, the unapprehensibility of Africa, offer the poetic voice a much more expansive poetic circumstance in which to play than the war-time Leeds settings (including a more serpentine syntax, less impelled by the rhymed line endings) this poetry is a poetry for the European to become upsettingly destabilized within:

The white wake swabbing at the greasy swell,
The swashing, greasy pool, the spindrift fine
As *Shelltox* seasoning my lips with brine
Makes sadness shoreless and shakes sullen grief
Apart like gobs of spittle.

('The Railroad Heroides', *SP* 27)

The neocolonial setting is thereby a gift to the recurrent theme of Harrison's early poems. At the same time, the specificity of the African setting is itself at times rather desperately clung to by the speakers in the poems, as an uncertain lexical sightline for what appear to be more existential crises that lose sight of the map, lose sight of 'Africa' and the spurious distinctions offered by Physical and Political geography:

Desperately I call these app-
rehensions Africa but the map
churns like wet acres in these rains
and thunder tugging at my veins.
That Empire flush diluted is
pink as a lover's orifice,
then *Physical, Political* run
first into marblings and then one
mud colour, the dirty, grey,
flat reaches of infinity.

The one red thing, I squat and grab
at myself like a one-clawed crab.

('The Foreign Body', *SP* 35)

Of course the colonial fact is returned to here: the fevered protagonist finds himself the sole embodiment of the flush of Empire red across, or upon, the map of Africa; but the delirious loss of the supposed political objectivity that makes a country mappable, knowable, colonizable is also suggested. And, as that suggestion is made, the poem closes. Desire needs a landscape upon which to write itself. In these poems the landscape of the African Other, and the loss of that terrain's knowability – while it enables a moment of virtuoso versification – returns the versifier sooner or later to a self-reflection that is a desperate clutching at his own and only strained heart. The most he can do is hold himself together. Africa extends without him.

The scenarios sketched out in the African poems, therefore, set

6

up a typically Harrisonian thematic mirror whereby the poems can be read as being as much 'about' the poetics of a colonialist inheritance (from the white neocolonialist's point of view) as they are 'about' the poetics of a discomforted, usually sexual, desire. At the same time one theme is an image of the other, each perpetually rubbing up against its counterpart with an inevitability and interminability that becomes more manic as the ex-pats' fear and ignorance becomes – in conjunction with a growing and desperate awareness of ageing and mortality – more self-reflexive. But this is a self-reflexiveness that, even as it draws the lexicon of the African landscape into the dialect of its own expression, its own remembering, perpetually returns to the fact of an unbreachable otherness, and thereby an experience of solipsism:

> It's you, it's you, with a sound like blood,
> After the bloodshed, if your tribe survives,
> Pounding a big man's yams among young wives.
>
> Leeds City Station, and a black man sweeps
> Cartons and papers into tidy heaps.

('The Railroad Heroides', SP 28)

There is love here, and a desperate love, and certainly something of an honourable acknowledgement of the demand for love ('There's love. There's courage. And that's all') that perpetually speaks through the fear and loathing of white lust in 'black Africa'. But even as the lust reads often enough as not so much an end in itself as some sort of blind gesture, any gesture at all, against 'this Nothingness [that] throbs in the blood', the expressed awareness, given by the poet to the European protagonists, of the fact of the European–African encounter as something of a punishing clash, damns that demand for love to a perpetually monological form. Africa remains with her back turned and her mouth closed – even as she is ventriloquised in the prophetic curse of Hieronymus Fracastorius (the poet born 'without a mouth') translated by Harrison into the centre of the monological sequence:

> You'll go on looking, losing more and more
> to the sea, the climate, weapons, ours *and* yours,
> your crimes abroad brought home as civil war.
>
> And also *Syphilis*: sores, foul sores
> will drive you back through storm and calenture
> crawling like lepers to our peaceful shores.

7

> The malaise of the West will lure
> the scapegoats of its ills, you and your crew,
> back to our jungles looking for a cure. –
>
> You'll only find the Old World in the New,
> and you'll rue your *discubrimiento*, rue
> it, rue Africa, rue Cuba, rue Peru!
>
> ('Distant Ophir', *SP* 29–30)

This curse, though, somewhat misses its mark if we consider it to be aimed in particular at its present translator and the author of these poems. 'Tony Harrison' both is – as in the unmediated naughtiness of 'The Zeg-Zeg Postcards (*'Mon égal!*/ Let me be the Gambia/ in your Senegal') – and is not, as elsewhere, complicit in the *discubrimiento* staged in these pieces. The sustained formality of his poetic structures alone, even as his characters succumb to 'tropical neurasthenia', sustains on his part a certain distance. Furthermore, the slippery (although at times brutally undiplomatic) diplomacy of the European–African encounter in these poems is exacerbated by what we might call the studied inconsistency of the poet's own relationship to his characters. Put simply, at times he occupies the first person, at times the third; but even the occupation of the first person is marked by a fastidiousness that raises the position of 'Tony Harrison' in all this as a question. For example, the songs of the PWD Man are characterized by an exuberance of *dramatis persona* that fixes the verses in the genre of the dramatic monologue: masks, theatrical impersonations:

> Though I'm not your socialistic, go-native-ite type chap
> With his flapping, nig-nog dresses and his dose of clap,
> I have my finer feelings and I'd like to make it clear
> I'm not just itchy fingers and a senile lecher's leer.
>
> (*SP* 42)

At the same time, the character's Leeds background, dialect and frame of reference marks him out as a Loiner proper, sprog of a peculiar culture to which Harrison himself claims allegiance. There is a sense at once of both distance and complicity, though distance wins out with the event of the PWD Man's death. The 'COND...COND...COND...' of the journey that survives the journeyer, the lines of condemned rusty coaltrucks accumulating like the bleeps on a cardiac monitor that registers a spent heart, as his

8

corpse is ferried back north, speaks a sad condemnation of the obsolescence of the character's type. On the other hand, in the verses where we get a more straightforwardly autobiographical persona, such as 'Heart of Darkness', we also get an absence of that lechery, apparent in other poems, which is directed primarily at a bit of the Other. Here the poet is with his wife, and although the imagery is again informed by a colonial historicism ('this blackout makes our flesh and bone/ an Africa, a Livingstone') the characters are surrounded by the tacky brought-over trappings of European Christian ceremony, and espoused in a verse dense with peculiarly Western literary allusions that mark it out as the poet's own and proper register. In fact it is this autobiographical-sounding poem that offers the one instance of Europeans suffering the objectifying, Othering gaze:

> Tuareg guards
> patrolling with their rusty swords
> swing up a lamp and weldmesh
> thief-bars check our flesh
> gleaming: breasts; thigh; bum;
> out of our aquarium.

(SP 39)

However, in those poems, such as *The White Queen* sequence, where the fetishizing gaze belongs to Europeans – and where that gaze is implicitly condemned as sad, self-immolating – Harrison occupies the first person with a tact that tempers sympathy with mistrust. There is something of a delay, during the half-serious disparaging self-imaging of the homosexual academic in the first poem of the sequence, before the 'I' is introduced. Perhaps the delay works as a fanfare, because certainly this first poem crescendoes to a positive celebration of boozy self-assertion. If, though, this character is to be taken as the narrator for the scenes that follow   some implicating the first person, others not – then the device is not pursued with dramatic consistency. This is particularly the case in sections iv and v, where the degree of intimacy and sympathy achieved in the portrayal of the 'lonely, unlovable old hag' and the 'sick MO' mitigate against ascribing these portraits to the speech of the White Queen himself. There is something in the dramatic distance, particularly in the African poems, between Harrison and his characters, that marks these

9

poems out, for all their bawdy, as a peculiarly tentative negotiation of the poetic I have been trying to describe. It is a particular form of tentativeness that will not be sustained for long.

At the risk of being reductive, we can suggest that the other early verses gathered in *Selected Poems* play variations on the themes outlined above by testing these dialectics with a variety of locations (and thus a variety of shades of political imperative) and a more committedly autobiographical utterance. A series of '[Red] Curtain' poems retwist the sex-love-in-foreign-parts theme by documenting the Prague courtship of a Czech-German girl by a rhyming English poet. 'Schwiegermutterlieder' reclaims the theme of how the cultural allegiance determined by location castigates the stolen love-match. Uncle Bertolt brings on his 1914–18 war wound stamping his foot against the marriage of his niece to an *'Engländer'*, but Uncle Bertolt is dying, on his way out, and the young English poet is gleefully incorporating Uncle's German words, along with his niece, and the trilled song of her Czech name, into his own lexicon. 'The Curtain Catullus' claims in its epigraph, after Yevtushenko, that it is 'frontiers' that 'oppress me.... I want to wander as much as I like... to talk, even in a broken language, with everybody'. A laudable ambition, perhaps, but it is the brokenness itself of a border-breaching language that appears to fascinate the speaker of these poems, the broken language and the apparently illicit sexual encounter with the East European Other that calls for the fashioning of this middle-European argot into poetry. Similarly laudable, on the face of it, is the defiant celebration of warm love in a Cold War climate:

> Come
> To my bugged bedroom. Leave mausoleum,
> Church, museum be. Leave your clothes there – Cold War
> Bashing its dead torches on our door.

There is also, though, something over-neat in such metaphorical oppositions that returns the poetry to a coldness, a cynicism even, that implicitly celebrates its capacity to incorporate the difficulties of historical contingency even as it overcomes those difficulties with metre and rhyme. In fact, the syntactic clumsiness of the example quoted immediately above betrays this impulse towards a neat metaphorical turn. Perhaps the epitome of this incorporation of metaphor is the sonnet 'Prague Spring'. Fortuitously, the poet's birthday falls on the eve of the Mayday marchpast. The occasion somehow seems to bequeath the proper location from which to view the Prague scene, beside a high-up gargoyle that seems to be 'puking his wassail on the listening throng' unless that same gargoyle is a frozen poet, hexed mid-song by the Medusa of Communism but about to thaw – and sing, the ice dribbling 'like spring saliva down his jaw'. Of course Harrison himself is not the gargoyle, he only borrows the statue's vantage, but the impressive metaphoric intricacy of the scene, marking liminality, transition, and masterful vantage all in four sentences and a mouthful of exclamations, claims, for this reader, too many prizes for the power of versification. Of course there is ambiguity here too, and that's an ambiguity that plays nicely in the short 'The Bedbug' where the speaker challenges the surveillance agent (and at the same time challenges the literary critic sniffing out degrees of insincerity in the poet's autobiographical utterance) to 'enter in the file which cry is real, and which/ A mere performance for your microphone'. But it is not an ambiguity that sustains the difficulty of the European–African encounters. Then again, maybe there is no reason that it should; and maybe, simply, the Middle-European scene is not as difficult – for the Englishman – as the African one. And, it should be added, remembering the sly admonition of 'The Bedbug', there are among these poems moments of deliberate provocation, moments of such audacious celebration of the poet's transubstantiation of the consumed Other into the matter of poetry, that challenge the attempt to damn contrivances.

So, in 'Guava Libre' he stages himself as Orpheus, the poet who goes down to Hades to bring back his dead wife Eurydice. In the old myth, of course, Orpheus fails to accomplish this, but Harrison goes 'down again', and again; and of course this going down is a figure for cunnilingus (in which the pleasure, as far as we hear about it here, is all his). The scene is simply him indulging in a jar of guavas soaked in Cuban rum, devising epithets by which to appropriate their shape and flavour, 'Pickled Gold Coast clitoridectomies?/ Labia minora in formaldehyde? [...] Lips cropped off a poet. That's more like.' If, meanwhile, the 'dykes' and feminist separatists holler offstage, the poet – or at least the persona by means of which he stages himself here – has an eye only to his own pleasure and the song that it will become. The gesture is, on the surface, one of a refusal to acknowledge (if such an acknowledgement means a sacrifice of a certain heterosexualized version of sensuality) the demands, contexts and determinants of the separatist agenda. And, on one level, the poet skates over certain political discomforts here as easily as does the *patineur* academic in the 'People's Palace' museum sliding between monuments of tsarist history. At the same time, though, there is an unambiguous politics in the present poem's frame of reference. Those 'clitoridectomies' speak loudly of an oppression that is violent, against sensuality, and specifically gendered in its violence. Thus, the lexicon of his poetic fantasy itself speaks against the freedom required, and taken, to speak that fantasy. The dialectic of pleasure and the price of pleasure is replayed here with a certain political nous. A mature staging, we might say, of a delighted sexual immaturity.

The poem that stretches that dialectic most outrageously in *The Loiners* is 'The Nuptial Torches' (*SP* 60–2). This is a monologue spoken by Isabella, Philip of Spain's bride, as she anticipates a process to the bridal bed illuminated by 'human victims, chained and burning at the stake.' The poem is a monstrous turn, exhibiting a Jacobean relish in the spectacle of cruelty it displays, and it is a relish that seems to belong as much, if not more so, to the poet behind the poem as to the frightened bride it ventriloquizes. The verses themselves, with all the lustre of Harrison's most vividly imagistic pentameters, seem to call applause for the poem's own *bons mots* after the fashion of the tyrant Philip himself. There is pity in the poem, certainly, and repulsion, and perhaps also an intimation of the payback to be returned for such sadistic indulgences, but these considerations operate, we might say, at the level of the poem's unconscious – or at the level of the modern reader's response (which may be the same thing). So, at the poem's proper linguistic surface, there is a tittering delight as an incongruous rhyme draws attention to the niceties of sixteenth-century costume together with basic physical repulsion at one

> Whose skin stinks like a herring in the sun,
> Huge from confinement in a filthy gaol,
> Crushing the hooping on my farthingale.

Or, if there is a resistance to the tortures described, it is for the sake simply of the speaker's own piece of mind:

> Let them lie still tonight, no crowding smoke
> Condensing back to men float in and poke
> Their charcoaled fingers at our bed, and let
> Me be his pleasure, though Philip sweat

Otherwise, there is the fantastic spectacle of the torches themselves:

> Their souls
> Splut through their pores like porridge holes.
> They wear their skins like cast-offs. Their skin grows
> Puckered round the knees like rumpled hose.

The uncertainty we might feel encountering such a poem, and which Harrison plays upon us so effectively, is to do with the fact that we cannot fully credit the poem's speaker with the sizzling verbal ingenuity that makes these verses memorable. Isabella is not, for example, a poet-persona in the way the White Queen, ostensible perpetrator of the 'Zeg-Zeg Postcards', was. Outside an integrated dramatic context, we do not altogether buy this poem as the deliberate speech of a *dramatis persona*. Therefore what gets staged, as throughout so much of *The Loiners*, is a hint of a claimed complicity, on the part of the poet, with the cruelties and oppressions that set off its scenes of sexual encounter. Perhaps we are in a poetic realm here shared with Yeats's 'Leda and the Swan', though where Harrison wins out, more or less, over Yeats's rape-scene, is in the avoidance of the phoney question ('Did she put on his knowledge with his power') that would seem to excuse the cruelty being staged. Harrison no-way excuses cruelty; rather he refuses to turn a blind eye to its contingency upon so many moments of human contact; and moreover, he omits any coyness in the depiction of this conjunction as fit matter for poetry. This omission – or more properly, refusal to omit – is becoming the measure of the political maturity of the poetic voice.

The last poems in *The Loiners*, following the trace of the poet's biography – he returned to Britain in 1967 at the age of 30 – return the poet, and his readers, to northern England (Newcastle and environs now rather than West Yorkshire), and bring home an accumulation and reconsideration of the themes and locations explored so far. As they do so, they exhibit an unambiguously autobiographical utterance – reminding us, thereby, of the autobiographical implications and complicities of even the proceeding persona poems. 'Newcastle is Peru' (*SP*, 63-8) declares a return in its first stanza, but this return is also a breaking down, of defences, of memories, of poses, and thus of the sufficient self:

> After Nigeria and Prague I come
> back near to where I started from,
> all my defences broken down
> on nine or ten *Newcastle Brown*.
>
> A sudden, stiff September breeze
> blows off the sea along the quays
> and chills us; autumn and I need
> your shoulder with a desperate need.

The next line, 'A clumsy effort at control', begins a process, ostensibly to light a fire (we shall see this particular Promethean figure return and return in the *oeuvre*), but also to regroup impetus, memory, persona from out of delirium into a deliberate poetry, and a celebratory poetry at that. Of course, the verses that unpack from here are anything but clumsy; but what with the 'detritus' that has to be raked out first, along with the Newcastle motto that heads the poem (given 'for defending in our Civil Wars/ The King's against the better cause') ingraining the new location with a history of uncomfortable complicity, not to mention the tricky metaphoric conceit that motors the poem (if Newcastle is Peru then anywhere is anywhere else, the poet's deliberate stanzas are belied by a shifting fictive geography), clumsiness and failure are written right through this self-accounting. The fire is lit with a newspaper urgent with stories of recent terrorist atrocities, and as this paper burns the poem acknowledges how the 'full-fledged bird of paradise' of its own chatter feeds and 'fattens on the voiceless dead'. Even this acknowledgement, however, is swept up into a vertigo, speeded by an unhalting syntax that barely has a moment for the silences that might punctuate self-reflection, as the verse itself replays 'a life-long, sick sixpennyworth/ of appalling motion round the earth', drawing all – Blackpool holidays, his first knee-trembler, Leeds funfairs, school, marriage, Africa, Prague – into the insatiable maw of poetic making, while the maker himself, unsteadily situated, looks drunkenly out over life and praises, as best he's able,

> each dark turn of the labyrinth
> that might like a river suddenly
> wind its widening banks into the sea
> and Newcastle is Newcastle is New-
> castle *is* Peru!

The fictive fact offers a moment's pause, and the rhythm of the poem at this point acknowledges that pause. The pause itself allows a collecting of thoughts for a more sober appreciation of the present scene, and any Peruvian attributes it might bear. However, the race is soon on again. Three stanzas are linked by first-word, last-word repetition (something like the 'forlorn' in Keats's ode on the nightingale that tolls him back to his sole self) and the link words, 'discovery' and 'rest', mark out the thematic dialectic of the verses that follow. The verse veers giddily between the heart and nerves of the poet, his situation, the 'us' he desires to draw down towards himself, and the labyrinthine maze of 'earth, people, planets' out there and undiscovered.[4] The poem reaches out to map that maze, as the hand, in love, reaches out to map the amazing body of the loved other, and whatever undiscovered countries are touched upon are found to be already marked with memory, with history, and with the 'grimy [...] smudge' of the poet's own experience, but then no less strange for all that. Newcastle *is* Peru. The scope of the poem's discovery is predetermined by the scope of the poet's own lexicon and image-kitty; but as whatever his accumulated inheritances add up to are drawn into the present, and this present is parsed out, through desire, into poetry, that same poetry glimpses its limits in silence, fear and death:

> Each whorl, my love-, my long life-line,
> mine, inalienably mine,
> lead off my body as they press
> onwards into nothingness.

The poem concludes with an image that packs the concerns of the whole volume (*The Loiners*) as if into a crucible, while returning that concatenation of themes back towards the reflective eye of the poet himself with a directness that has hardly been encountered elsewhere among these early verses:

> And I'm left gazing at a full-page spread
> of aggressively fine bosoms, nude
> and tanned almost to *négritude*,
> in the Colour Supplement's *Test*
> *Yourself for Cancer of the Breast.*

Our themes so far: an ostensibly autobiographical organization of material that appropriates places, people, experiences as if they delivered a lexicon, the lexicon of a landscape that has been scanned, fed upon, put into; a lexicon that constitutes the developing dialect with which the poet's first person measures his growing up into his vocation – a vocation which might be characterized as developing a technology for the expression of love.

We need here to step over the *School of Eloquence* sequence (those poems will be considered in another place) and look briefly – too briefly, but space permits little more – at pieces at the other end of *Selected Poems*. These are poems set in the American scene, scene of a happy marriage, and a scene in which the poet cultivates, and consumes, the fruit of a successful career. Of course that fruit is not uniformly sweet. Harrison declares his adoption of the kumquat as 'the fruit right for my prime' which, with its 'sweet pulp and sour skin'

> expresses best
> how days have darkness round them like a rind,
> life has a skin of death that keeps its zest.
>
> (*SP* 193)

The poet's wisdom is to know himself now 'an older not a wiser man', but the unknown that borders upon his 'Being' is no longer the books not read, the people not met, the places yet unvisited, but the unknowable 'Nothingness' of death: 'Man's Being ripened by his Nothingness'. The poet's wisdom is to know the unspeakability of that Non-Thing: note those empty parentheses in 'The Heartless Art', the elegy for his friend Seth Tooke that admits to 'the final failure of the poet' (*SP* 208). Even so he continues to draw the weave of his poetry from the landscape he lives upon; but the flora of these scenes, comprehending the poet's wisdom, is sown between culture and (apparent) nature: the thing uprooted for the cultivation of man's habitat, and the merely organic thing that grows and dies. Here we have the flowers ingeniously fashioned into the floats at Pasadena's New Year Rose Parade that, 'next day', succumb, 'to seconds and to Centigrade' ('Skywriting', *SP* 196–8). Here we have the 'Juniper, aspen, blue spruce' and pine that grow around D. H. Lawrence's abode in New Mexico, almost overwhelmed by the deadening commodification of both the poet and the Navajo natives that are, themselves, forgotten, literally pissed on, by the signs of that commodification ('The Call of Nature', *SP* 199). Here we have 'the Old World's edibles' petrified in a Washington statue of the Horn of Plenty ('All that motherly bounty turned to stone!') while urban demolition continues apace, and American foreign policy and institutionalized racism and violence at home comprehends the extinction of peoples ('The Red Lights of Plenty', *SP* 203–5). Here we have the poet filling a hole with a compost of confused organic matter, 'hackberry leaves, pine needles, stuff like that', while his friend dies inside the house: 'Next spring [...] we'll have the land grassed over and quite flat' ('The Heartless Art'). Here we have the organization of property: the cultivation of fire-gaps at the front of the house, the non-cultivation of 'wilderness' at the back. The 'cracker', red-neck neighbour blasts at snakes and alligators on his land ('The Lords of Life', *SP* 209–13). The liberal poet on his plants a pine-hedge, as a 'demarcation' of his property, but also as a shield behind which he and his wife can tend their saplings in the nude, like some protected species out of a dream of D. H. Lawrence's ('Following Pine', *SP* 220–29). And, as the poet describes this last landscape and its careful cultivation, and calls it his, and celebrates it, and declares an intention to live in it, he remembers that pine is cut for both the floorboards of newlyweds and the coffins of the dead. The last two lines of this last poem draw around the poet and his wife a close landscape, an enclosure for living in (fun in the nude) and for no-longer living in (when all our earthly cares are cast off). The world still makes its contribution to the lexicon of love, but the dialect of the poet will have found its proper privacy:

> A morning incense smokes off well-doused ground.
> Everywhere you water rainbows shine.
> This private haven that we two have found
> might be the more so when enclosed with pine.

2

Translations

Harrison's work as a poet is informed by the interests and discipline of the scholar, as demonstrated in his exemplary fastidiousness (I believe lovers of the works will grant the point), and also in his dedication to a learning project that we could fairly describe as archaeological. This scholarship is evidenced in the range and depth of his learning, and all those unfamiliar words that ensure that the present critic, at least, writes these pages with a hefty dictionary to hand. It is also evidenced, however (partly *through* that unfamiliar lexicon, that digging up) in terms that I have already attempted to delineate with the phrase 'political imperative'. That imperative is to do, among other things, with paying respect to the dead, with material analysis of the remains of human cultures, as well as the unearthing of the unconscious (in the psychoanalytic sense), and the silenced: the repressed and the oppressed. It is not, though, a project solely concerned with the past. The unearthing and bringing to light of signs and their meanings (or histories of meaning) is involved in the issue of how to survive in the present. The epigraph to *v.* gives us a clue:

> My father still reads the dictionary every day. He says your life depends on your power to master words.

> (Arthur Scargill, *Sunday Times*, 10 January 1982)

The quoting of the National Union of Mineworkers leader around the time of the divisive coal-strike in Britain is one mark of political allegiance. Also involved here, however, is the more general issue of the necessity of a scholarship that allows one to participate in the power-processes of the application, comprehension and contestation of signifying practices. The fastidiousness mentioned above, then, is vital. This project of learning, and the sharing of learning, is not something separate from Harrison's

18

work as a poet. It is integral. I shall explore Harrison's 'archaeological' learning project in the present chapter by making a few comments on his work as a translator.

If we are to say that Harrison's scholarship shines through his poetry, we need also to mention that his personal and political investment in the work he signs his name to shines through his translations. Tony Harrison is hardly ever what we might call an 'invisible' translator. His translation work perpetually draws attention to the active presence and role of the translator within the complex series of negotiations that translation involves, although this role may not be the same from work to work. Some of the most obvious examples of a drawing attention to the fact of the translator come in Harrison's prefatory material: moments where he makes a statement about what is at stake, for him, in the texts and the conditions under which they were produced. As a brief and, for the moment, general example, a poem by Bertolt Brecht's collaborator, Leon Feuchtwanger, 'Adaptations', which is printed at the head of *Theatre Works 1973–1985*, opens with an apparently unambiguous authorial 'I' ('I, for instance, sometimes write/ Adaptations') before going on to make problematic mileage out of questions such as: Who is the author of this work? Who deserves the final credit? How might a translator or adaptor be 'respectful' to their source? What is the difference between translation and adaptation? How 'dead' is a 'dead author'?:

> *The dead writer's failures*
> *Will be ascribed*
> *To me and all my successes*
> *To the dead writer who is extremely*
> *Famous and quite unknown, and of whom*
> *Nobody knows whether he himself*
> *Was the writer or maybe the*
> *Adaptor.*

The answers to such questions remain up for grabs, but the poem (which is itself a translation, of course: is that 'I' Feuchtwanger's or Harrison's?) has already done more for the reader than simply draw attention to the labour of a translator or adapter. It encourages us to think of the translator as someone who is peculiarly positioned between different texts, different cultural contexts and historical moments, different audiences and readerships, and is

19

therefore making a series of particular choices and decisions. A more particular example is the brief preface to the 1981 translations from the Roman poet Marcus Valerius Martialis (Martial) collected in *U.S. Martial* where Harrison describes the stone head of a satyr that overlooked the New York hotel room where he completed his 'labours'. A photograph of this satyr appears on the cover of the collection, and the diabolically gleeful grin on that stone face suggests that the transformation of these poems from first-century Latin to 1980s American vernacular has been presided over by a personality that was no way neutral or self-effacing, a personality with an inscrutable agenda of their own. However, a third sort of example of the visibility – or perhaps I should say audibility – of the translator in his work comes not from Harrison himself, but from his audience, or at least his critics. The selection of press reviews of *The Misanthrope* gathered in Astley's critical anthology all draw attention to how Harrison's own work on Molière's play was one of the most prominent aspects of whatever it was that was striking about the show. So, from Benedict Nightingale's column in the *New Statesman*:

> Instead of wondering just how [Alec] McCowen's Alceste or Diana Rigg's Célimène would react to this or that twist of the plot, [the audience] was almost audibly asking itself what striking new rhyme Harrison would wrest out of the original text, what epigram he would concoct from the references to *Figaro*, the Elysée, Special Powers Act, skiing [. . .]. (Astley, 155)

None of which is mentioned for the sake of a simplistic point about Harrison deliberately overshadowing his source texts with his own writing. Rather, I wish to offer the argument that for Harrison the issue of fidelity to the translator's task is much more than a case of finding equivalent English phrases and images for the source text, if such a thing were possible at all. The options available to a translator are hardly as self-evident as that. In fact, it seems that there are so many contexts and decisions for the translator to negotiate – decisions that, it would be fair to say, amount in effect to a politics of translation – that for a translator to pretend that his own self-effacement or 'invisibility' were possible would be in itself an evasion of his professional and political responsibility.

The case can, I hope, be made clearer by indulging in a brief scholarly moment of my own, and comparing Harrison's work with certain academic theories of translation. In a recent overview of such theories, Romy Heylen argues that translation is 'above all, a form of cultural negotiation', and 'should not be seen as a rule-regulated activity but a decision-making process'.[1] One upshot of this is that the translator is understood to be working with particular objectives in mind that are likely to be as much political as they are 'merely' literary. We should not, that is, think of translation as a process in which one blindly follows a set of mechanical rules for the sake of finding 'equivalences', synonyms, and identities between different languages. Such a process, I suggest, might be akin to the Latin translation classes that Harrison remembers, with horror, from his schooldays: 'I remember once making a policeman in a Plautus play say something like "*Move along there*", only to have it scored through and "*vacate the thoroughfare*" put in its place' (Astley, 139). Neither, though, is Harrison suggesting here that one follow another obligation to translate old languages into contemporary, 'living', vernacular. That would only be another orthodoxy. Rather it is a case of recognizing the political implications of the decisions that a translator must *choose* to make, out of all the options available – including linguistic and performative options that do not even become available to poets, directors and actors until the translation process, the establishing of new relationships between languages and cultures, is entered into. In Heylen's phrase, translation is a 'profoundly transformative' process. In Harrison's own phrases, in the course of a preface to his translation of *The Misanthrope*, and in the context of a meditation on Walter Benjamin's essay on the translator's task:

> Translations are not built to survive though their original survives through translation's many flowerings and decays. The illusion of pedantry is that a text is fixed. It cannot be fixed once and for all. The translation is fixed but reinvigorates its original by its decay. It was probably on these lines that Walter Benjamin was thinking when he said in his *The Task of the Translator* that 'the life of an original reaches its ever-recurring, latest and most complete unfolding in translations'. (Astley, 146)[2]

The translator is effecting a series of differences, of shifts; and the decisions and choices involved are bound by all sorts of particular contexts and goals. So, the translator is not simply translating *into* another language (not to mention into a new social and cultural context, with its own sets of values, its own ways of disseminating, receiving and evaluating texts and their meanings), but also into new relationships *between* texts, between languages, between cultural contexts. To take the minor example of the school lesson quoted above, the politics of the translator's art might involve the issue of contesting (*or* choosing to conform to) current understandings of how, say, a culture perceives its own relationship to 'classic' texts. Or, to highlight another aspect of the same issue, that same classic text may as much be a pretext for challenging what sort of language, what sort of dialect has validity on an English-language stage, as much as it offers an opportunity for a (re)consideration of the translated text itself. Thus – and we are back with Heylen's arguments here – the politics of translation straddles issues of cultural conformity and cultural resistance; the work of translation stages a series of political negotiations, and is not simply 'the result of a crossing of linguistic barriers'.[3]

As I have already begun to suggest, translation involves much more than merely linguistic issues, especially for Tony Harrison. Translation is as much a thematic of his work as it is a practical aspect of his professional activity, and to the extent to which the activity is a process of cultural negotiation we might include within its purlieus the analogical use made by the poet of the sexual encounters narrated in *The Loiners*; the fantastic geographical transplantation of Newcastle to Peru (and vice versa); the digging out of marinaded guavas into metaphors for the sexual politics of the poet's art; let alone those actual translations gathered in the 'Travesties' section of *The White Queen*; in all of which we see a perpetually renegotiated story of cultural shift, of the power-relations and compromises implied in a whole series of particular interactions between cultures, ethnicities, sexes, genders, languages, and historical and political perspectives. Furthermore, through the dramatic use of the first person persona in these poems, and the placing of a certain amount of culpability upon that persona for intercultural betrayals and misunderstandings, Harrison stages his theme as an ongoing problem, drawing readers' attention as much to the roads not travelled (politically speaking) by his globe-trotting muse as to the achievement evidenced by the completed poems.

Even further, if all Harrison's translations and adaptations, both metaphoric and literal, are written over by the first-person persona, the 'I' that announces his responsibility for, or dramatizes his own evasion of the responsibilities attendant upon these various negotiations, we are justified in noting the peculiarly performative nature of the translator's activity. This is to say more than simply most of this poet's translations are written for the theatre. It is to include, we might even suggest, a comic perspective on his work, as Harrison himself does when, in one of the prefaces to *The Misanthrope*, he describes the Victorian academic anthropologist measuring the 'endowments' of the so-called 'Hottentot Venus' (an African woman shipped over to Imperial Britain as an ethnic curiosity) in terms of trigonometry and logarithms. Harrison's own riposte is that today 'the poet, and the man of the theatre, have to be bolder and more intimate' (Astley, 140). Of course the comedy of this anecdote barely makes explicit the history of sexual and ethnic oppression involved in it, but it goes far enough, through implications that succeed in accessing racism and misogyny in the same breath, in erasing any claims for methodological neutrality on the part of the translator who might be heard to speak through the 'travesties' (to refer back to the title of Harrison's 'African' group of verse translations) of his texts. The position from which the translator speaks is always an issue, he comes on stage when his texts are spoken and is never the least significant actor in the drama that is played out there.

Let us, allowing for how much of Harrison's translation work has been done for theatre, suggest that, in all his translations – theatrical and otherwise – he approaches the work in terms of the writing of a drama. That is to say Harrison translates what appear to be speaking voices, and the contexts in which voices speak, rather than the dead letter of authors' texts. Further to this, though, the translations include within their form and verbal texture a dramatization of the interpretive distance that we, as readers, and Harrison as translator, must take from these voices. I shall take the non-theatrical examples first, the translations from the Greek of the fourth-century Alexandrian poet Palladas, collected in *Palladas: Poems* (reprinted in *Selected Poems*); and those from the Latin poet Martial rendered into New York vernacular in *U.S. Martial* (1981, not collected in present editions of *Selected Poems*). Palladas's is a particular idiosyncratic voice, and Harrison has attempted to present in his selection 'a consistent dramatic personality' (Astley, 134). We might say that

23

the Palladas texts evidence an *idiolect*, an archaeological project indeed, these epigrams from the Greek Anthology set as if in aspic, trumpeting alone 'the last hopeless blasts of the old Hellenistic world' (Astley, 134). The Martial poems, on the other hand, exercise a *dialect*, the speech of a speech-*community*. The difference is significant.

In spite of the accessible modernity into which Harrison translates Palladas's voice ('all that "immortality" and "divine life" stuff', *SP* 77), that voice, that dramatic personality, seems exhumed rather than updated. Palladas, with his fatalistic last-ditch Paganism, ranting against the new Christian culture that is already, in his own lifetime, making the culture he has grown up in obsolete, is a ghost in our world. Sure, we can relate to him, enjoy him, and he is given the opportunity to speak with clarity in Harrison's version, but we do not feel that we could enter a dialogue with him. In short, although Harrison is making Palladas accessible and believable to us, and although he finds a vernacular speech and images of social context that serve to bring Palladas's world to light, it is as if Harrison has also succeeded in translating a modern reader's *distance* from that context.

> Knocked off his pedestal! THEY've
> done *this* to Heracles?
> Flabbergasted I began to rave
> and went down on my knees:
>
> *Giant, whose birth took three whole days,*
> *whose image stands at each crossroad,*
> *you to whom the whole world prays,*
> *our Champion, KOed?*
>
> That night he stood at my bed-end
> and smiled and said: *I can't complain.*
> *The winds of change are blowing, friend,*
> *your god's a weather-vane.*
>
> (*SP* 92)

Those upper-case letters and italics in the first two lines give a strong impression of this being a real, living voice, and phrases like 'flabbergasted' and 'KOed' are contemporary English slang, they bring Palladas convincingly into a modern reader's known world. However, Palladas's concern with the passing of Greek Pagan culture is not something we can relate to so easily, and the

24

poem itself, through the ghost of Heracles, allows that this was already becoming the case in Palladas's own day ('the winds of change are blowing'). Harrison's achievement here is a complex one, to bring the character to life, as it were, while simultaneously persuading us that we must encounter him as the representative of a lost and forgotten world.

This sense of exhumation is elaborated by Harrison littering his version with Anglo-Saxonisms that are already non-current in our own vernacular. 'Thole the pain', says Palladas (*SP* 77), and that old word for 'suffer' speaks a belligerent old-fashionedness both of vernacular and attitude. Our appreciation of them as archaeological drama is exacerbated by the fact that although the Palladas pieces are indeed epigrams, short, pungent, satirical pieces, they come across much more as tone of voice, as attitude, than verbal wit:

> Born crying, and after crying, die.
> It seems the life of man's just one long cry.

> (*SP* 77)

There's a joke there of sorts in that couplet, but wit takes second place to wry bitterness. Further, the whole sequence seems like a series of notebook jottings, put into rhyme for the sake of making them memorable to the writer, little summings-up of a point of view, mnemonics for an attitude – as if that attitude might even be forgotten by the speaker in his changing world, as if he has to make these compressed comments so as to hold onto his sense of the world. But this is not a sense that we can necessarily join in with. Sometimes the witticisms are so peculiar they come across as a joke that Palladas could only share with himself or other grammarians:

> A grammarian's daughter had a man
> then bore a child m. f. & n.

> (*SP* 84)

Palladas's voice has survived the world in which it circulated, and there is a pathos there. There is an irony here also that, to the extent to which it is a knowing irony of the speaker's, speaks back against his own attitudes, and all this makes him a fine dramatic character, but a character in a rather tragic drama, strung out, as Harrison writes in his preface, over the choice between 'a crumbled past and a future of specious regeneration' (Astley, 134). As analogy this is perhaps a tragedy we can relate to, but what Harrison has done is textualize this dilemma through his dramatic mode of translation, by setting Palladas's poems to a custom-built idiolect.

The translations from the Roman poet Marcus Valerius Martialis (AD *c.* 40–*c.*104), *U.S. Martial,* constitute a very different sort of achievement. As I've already mentioned, in a short preface to the collection Harrison writes that he completed these translations within a few days, in a New York hotel room overlooking the stone head of a satyr that both seemed to look into the room where he was working while at the same time 'taking in the multifarious life of New York City and missing nothing'. The stone satyr might remind us of the gargoyle in the earlier sonnet 'Prague Spring', possessing a vantage point over a much wider and, obviously, more current scene than that scanned by Palladas. We think of Harrison sharing this satyr's vantage, high above the city, not so much translating a single voice from the book in front of him, but picking up on the airwaves, as it were, from the city below, scraps from all sorts of voices. Again Harrison is translating Classical literature into a vernacular (an American one this time) but now he is giving us a speech *community* rather than an idiolect which would be the speech of a particular character. Furthermore these voices do not belong to the past so much as to the present day of modern New York. Harrison's comment that he wrote the sequence in a 'few days' is helpful. It is as if these short poems are snatched out of the air as they are spoken, before they are lost; and they do not contain any complex wit, they are not to be poured over with the reverence due to Literature. Nor do they even seem to be the work of an author altogether, rather they seem overheard, as if they are scraps of larger conversations which the English poet is not quite party to. The poems are bitchy, trivial, concerned with individuals' peculiar foibles and sexual dealings.[4] This is cocktail party chat:

> *She* wants more and more and more new men in her.
>
> *He* finally finishes *Anna Karenina.*
>
> (XVI, 'The Joys of Separation')

The 'wit' appears at first to be simply in the rhyme itself, as if the comment is asking only for a chuckle of applause for a well-turned phrase from the fellow party-goers it is spoken to, all of whom belong to the same social circle as 'her' and 'him', this recently separated couple who are finding different ways to fill their newly found spare time. And of course Tolstoy's nineteenth-century novel *Anna Karenina* was not a reference available to the first-century poet Martial; rather it is a point of reference (a coded reference to adultery perhaps) appropriate to chatty, educated modern city-dwellers. Martial's poem has been used as a pretext to ventriloquize a comment that might be made, in jest, today. Made, and then forgotten. It seems to be nudge nudge wink wink stuff, no more, and to that extent entertaining enough; although if we look at the couplet for a little longer than it seems to demand we find a story packed in there of some little pathos. Those 'joys of separation' are not *altogether* joys. The man who has finished Tolstoy's novel has a *lot* of solitary time, and his 'ex' hardly seems to be finding any *lasting* satisfaction. It is the way that such a poem encourages us to read such a scenario into it that allows us to note the way it seems projected at a speech-community that will readily pick up on its terms, people who might remember their own inability to plough through Tolstoy's tome; who might recall their own inclination to celebrate a holiday from monogamy in similar fashion; or who will appreciate the joke to the extent to which they share the speaker's urbane (misogynistic) attitudes.

And nor do we get the sense, as we did with the Palladas pieces, that all the poems are spoken by the same person:

> You're fucking Aufidia, your ex
> who's married to the guy who gave *you* grounds.
> Adultery's the one way you get sex.
> You only get a hard-on out of bounds.
>
> (VIII)

The range of concerns (other people's sex lives) and mode of expression are similar in both pieces so far quoted, but it is a similarity of type, rather than of a particular voice. There is no idiolect as such. If the Palladas translations sufficed to stage the pathos of the Greek poet's own predicament in the present un-Hellenistic age, the Roman Classic will serve as an interventionary comment on the pathetic eddies of energy in certain pockets of our own contemporary urban decadences. The translator is heard behind all this both as a voice (we have become familiar with a peculiarly Harrisonian epigrammatic style, we have a sense of the jokes he likes to chuckle at), but also as a politicized intelligence, measuring how these 'originals' *can* be heard in the present moment – a moment that, for readers of the present text, may anyway already be gone.

Translating into the present 'moment' has been a particular issue with Harrison's theatre work, and the pertinence of a translation is no less a determinant of that translation's subsequent redundancy than it is of its effectivity in the moment of its staging. Harrison happily allows for that redundancy:

> It seems to me now, after the experience of creating a version of the Lysistrata for Nigerian actors (unplayable outside West Africa) and of *Le Misanthrope* for the National, that the best way of creating a fresh text of a classic is to tie it to a specific production rather than aim, from the study, at a general all-purpose repertory version.

> (Astley, 144)

That Nigerian version of Aristophanes' comedy *Lysistrata* was *Aikin Mata*, co-adapted with the Irish poet James Simmons, and performed at Ahmadu Bello University, Zaria, in March 1964. Harrison has tackled *Lysistrata* again since, in *The Common Chorus*, a trilogy of plays set at the USAF base at Greenham Common, but since the Greenham Common issue has been passed over by events the trilogy has remained unperformed.[5] 'A "classic"', though, 'needs to be retranslated continuously.' No particular version can claim to stand as the best or the definitive version, and Harrison's work, in preparing texts for specific productions, has been as much in structuring the terms of the encounter between a play and a particular audience as it has been in the replacing of a speech in one language with a speech in another.

So, with *Aikin Mata*, the objectives involved finding, in the first instance, a non-Nigerian play that addressed current cultural issues in Nigeria such as the sex war between men and women, and which employed theatrical conventions similar to modern Nigerian classics such as Wole Soyinka's *The Lion and the Jewel*; then finding for that play a linguistic division peculiar to Nigerian culture that mirrored the division between the 'received pronunciation' of Attic Greek and the 'sub-standard' Doric Greek of the Spartans in the Aristophanes original (Harrison and Simmons employed a conflict between north Nigerian

'Standard' English and the Pidgin spoken in the south).[6] In the translation of Molière's *Le Misanthrope* for the National Theatre in England, Harrison 'translated' the setting for the drama from the mid-seventeenth-century French Court of Louis XIV to the autocratic 'Cour' of De Gaulle in the 1960s. The objective here was not to update the references so as to say something more 'relevant' about *French* culture, but to aim, in a sort of working marriage between the original text and the translated text, at a diagnosis of certain sorts of self-righteous critiques of social corruption (such as Alceste's outbursts in the play) that considers the failure of political potential in such critiques, in any culture, including our own (Astley, 147–9). The fidelity to Molière is not so much in the retention of the French dramatist's words and images (although Harrison *is* remarkably faithful in this respect in this particular work) but in preserving an ambiguity of political analysis, and making that ambiguity readable for a London theatre audience in 1973. With Racine's *Phèdre* (translated as *Phaedra Britannica* and performed by the National Theatre at the Old Vic in 1975) Harrison went further than mere updating, transposing Racine's own transposition of Euripides' Greek drama to British India under the Raj, and taking, along the way, a much greater liberty with Racine's lexicon and versification than he had with Molière's. The issue here was 'to rediscover a *social* structure which makes the tensions and polarities of the play significant again' (Astley, 175). What had to be staged here, in a way in which the show's audience could see and hear it, was a particular dialectical tension between fascination and repression, civilization and its discontents. In particular Harrison was faced with the problem of making the central *donnée* of the play – Memsahib's (Phèdre's) illicit lust for her stepson, Thomas (Hyppolite) – *matter*. Harrison had to 'consider solutions to the play which would place the problem in a society where the sense of transgression was once more an agonising burden' (Astley, 185). The translation, then, involved more even than the transposition to the Raj setting. For example, Harrison writes in his preface of how the energies of a particular famous line ('*La fille de Minos et de Pasiphaé*' – it is hard for a modern audience, British or otherwise, to unpack the ideological allusions in those mythological names) had to be redistributed over the whole version in an extended nexus of imagery so that the social,

29

political and psychological tensions expressed in that one line might be given back to the contemporary theatre. In short, he restages Racine's drama of fetishization by tapping into the spectres of neocolonial fantasy in the imaginations of his post-colonial audience, replaying, at white heat, in the historicized fantasy of an 'alien' scene, the tensions between rigid moral and social codes and transgressive sexual desire.

With *The Oresteia* (performed at the Royal National Theatre in 1981 and the ancient theatre of Epidaurus in 1982) the objectives and attendant decisions were again different. There was little, it seems, in this production to do with transposing the *mise-en-scène* for the sake of relevance or readability. The drama itself, of 'a society truly debating with itself' was relevance enough.[7] Even the Greek titles of the individual plays were retained. The issue now – which had to be worked out over a ten-year gestation period of collaboration between Harrison, Hall, and the composer Harrison Birtwistle – was one of linguistic texture, of poetry proper. This issue, for Harrison, is nothing less than relevant, or political:

> Regular rhythm, form in poetry is like the mask it enables you to go beyond the scream as a reaction to events that in the normal course of life would make you do just that. Our century is very much in need of it. (Astley, 280)

The bottom-line objective was always to produce a text that lent itself to performance, to speakability. As Harrison's own note to the trilogy insists, 'This text is written to be performed, a rhythmic libretto for masks, music, and an all-male company' (*TW*, 187). The text as we have it is staggering, although unfortunately the present writer was too young, too impecunious, too far from London (or Epidaurus) to see the stage production. What is striking, though, about the text – and this is brought out in that brief selection of Harrison's correspondence with Hall – is the extent to which Harrison's work seems (I don't read Greek either, Greek was not obligatory at Leeds Grammar School in my day) to have been a deliberate *return* to Aeschylus's Greek poetry. It is as if previous translations had become accretions upon the original, masking what Roland Barthes (in a discussion of the ways that photography can 'prick' me, touch me, moving me to enter 'crazily into the spectacle, into the image, taking into my arms what is dead, what is going to die') described as the *punctum* of the aesthetic object.[8] These accretions had not, though, become the mask of 'poetry', referred to above, 'the door of the metal mask of the palace' behind which the scream itself is about to be heard (Astley, 280). None of these other translations seemed 'even remotely playable except in the flimsiest fragments' (Astley, 275). So, Harrison went back to Aeschylus. 'In the end I just went back to the Greek' (Astley, 277). He went back to

> Aeschylean modes of image making and neologising to use wherever they occur to me or seem effective in English, so that I extract a certain stylistic principle and allow it to be distributed over the version. (Astley, 277)

These neologisms were married to the alliteration and caesura, and occasional ballad metre of old English poetry, but all in the service of a fidelity to the performability of Aeschylus's verse. The dialogue exchanges of the 'stychomythia' were made rhymed and formal, and tendencies towards a naturalistic speech in early drafts of the dialogues that punctuate the choruses and set speeches were excised because 'we must never in the whole piece be let off the rhythmical hook, *never*' (Astley, 279). And the result? As most commentators on Harrison's translations tend to do at this point, I offer, but without comment, a series of brief comparative samples, and refer the reader to the irreducible whole of Harrison's version, the whole of Aeschylus's trilogy. The samples are from a speech of Clytemnestra's in *The Agamemnon*. Firstly from Richard Lattimore's version:

> The sea is there and who shall drain its yield? It breeds
> precious as silver, ever of itself renewed,
> the purple ooze wherein our garments shall be dipped.
> And by God's grace this house keeps full sufficiency
> of all. Poverty is a thing beyond its thought.
> I could have vowed to trample many splendours down
> had such decree been ordained by the oracles
> those days when all my study was to bring home your life.
> For when the root lives yet the leaves will come again
> to fence the house with shade against the Dog Star's heat.[9]

From Louis MacNeice's version:

> There is the sea and who shall drain it dry? It breeds
> Its wealth in silver of plenty of purple gushing
> And ever-renewed, the dyeings of our garments.

31

The house has its store of these by God's grace, King.
This house is ignorant of poverty
And I would have vowed a pavement of many garments
Had the palace oracle enjoined that vow
Thereby to contrive a ransom for his life.
For while there is root, foliage comes to the house
Spreading a tent of shade against the Dog Star.[10]

And finally Harrison:

The sea's there for ever. No one can drain it.
And it oozes for ever the dyes of dark sea-red
to stain all the garments this house has wealth of.
The gods have made sure that we've never been lacking.
And if gods had prescribed it as a rite for his safety
I would have trampled each inch of rich raiment.
If the treeroot's living the house gets new leafage
spreading cool shade at the time of the dogstar.

(TW 213)

None of which is to imply that linguistic texture had not been an issue in Harrison's earlier translations for the theatre. In the preface to *The Misanthrope* the poet speaks, for example, of the problem thrown up by English having 'a greater degree of physical concretisation' than French (Astley, 143). In that play, he had striven for a degree of colloquialism, but interestingly he was able to achieve something of this, by specifically lexical rather than syntactic means, when a production decision was taken by the director, John Dexter, to do the play in 'modern*ish* dress'. This decision, peculiar to that production, enabled the updating of the *mise-en-scène* described above, but also enabled the translator to employ a specific lexical and syntactic charge in his lines, a charge he could set off against what he has called the ticking 'time-bomb' of Molière's rhyming couplet (Astley, 140). In the Racine play, however, he wanted 'a more organic model' for the verse. In line with the particular dramatic objectives already described, 'I wanted to return the iamb back to its sources in breath and blood' (Astley, 191). One could extend the discussion with details and examples, but I want to conclude this too-brief survey of Harrison's translation work with a few comments on *The Mysteries* (performed at the Royal National Theatre and at the Lyceum Theatre in 1985, and televised over Christmas 1985–6 by Channel 4), Harrison's adaptations, done in collaboration with the

National Theatre Company, from the Middle Ages cycles of plays: York, Towneley (from Wakefield), Chester and the *Ludus Coventriae* ('Coventry's play'). Harrison's structural achievement in adapting all this material to an integral cycle of his own has already been discussed by Bernard O'Donoghue, a commentator much more qualified to speak on these matters than myself.[11] I only want here to expand upon Harrison's much-quoted comment in a prefatory note to the Faber edition of his cycle, that his role in the production was as 'a Yorkshire poet who came to read the metre and to monitor the preservation of the plays' Northern character'. We return here to what I attempted to characterize, at the head of this essay, as an archaeological scholarship, but now it needs insisting that we do not mean by that, to quote one of Harrison's comments on preparing the *Oresteia* text, 'being in the reproduction furniture or restoration drama business' (Astley, 278). The implication in the comment from the metre-man above is that the metre has been ticking over fine, thank you, for a long time, even if nobody has been paying the bill. It has been ticking over, largely, in northern English vernacular speech, of which the medieval plays form one written archive, and Harrison's published versions (monitoring the preservation, the continuity) another. Tom Paulin characterizes vernacular (literature) as

> a speech packed with 'sentence sounds', sounds which writers gather 'by the ear from the vernacular' [...] an ecstatic tribal innocence that suddenly breaks the surface-rhythm like a shoal of fry [...] the intoxication of speech, its variety and crack and hilarity.[12]

We find this tribal innocence, this crack and hilarity, alive and well – as far as literature ever is that – in the fruitiest moments of the original Mystery plays, such as the 'Second Shepherds' Pageant' (*Secunda Pastorun*) from the Towneley Cycle. The sheep-stealer Mak has entered with a rich cloak covering his tunic:

> *Mak.* What! ich be a yeoman, I tell you, of the kyng,
> The self and the some, sond from a greatt lordyng,
> And sich.
> Fy on you! Goyth hence
> Out of my presence!
> I must haue reuerence.
> Why, who be ich?
> *1 Pastor.* Why make ye it so qwaynt? Mak, ye do wrang.

33

2 Pastor. But, Mak, lyst ye saynt? I trow that ye lang.
3 Pastor. I trow the shrew can paynt, the dewyll myght hym hang!
Mak. Ich shall make complaynt, and make you all to thwang
At a worde,
And tell euyn how ye doth.
1 Pastor. Bot, Mak, is that sothe?
Now take outt that Sothren tothe,
And sett in a torde!
2 Pastor. Mak, the dewill in youre ee! A stroke wold I leyne you.
3 Pastor. Mak, know ye not me? By God, I couthe teyn you.
Mak. God looke you all thre! Me thoght I had sene you.
Ye are a fare compané.[13.]

Only a little amount of effort with the dictionary gives us access to the voices rehearsed in those texts, and allows some of us (if not all), I believe, to recognize something there – in one of those myopic dehistoricizing gestures of appropriation that we make, as readers of literature, when we want to say we 'love' this thing – that we can claim as our own. Such gestures anyway, I would argue, are validated by the experience in the theatre when literature is made 'live' by being spoken by the actor, present and before us. Harrison tunes into that gesture. He barely, in places, updates the ancient lexicon. He lets it sing, if not on its own terms, then on terms that it marks out itself, anew, afresh, in the moment of performance. Is this translation? Is this adaptation?[14] In the theatre, without our Old English Texts beside us, who can tell? Who cares? The translator scholar returns to the words and returns the words to the poet, who turns all over to the world to take as it pleases:

MAK
What! I be a yeoman, I tell you, of the king's,
The selfsame one, messenger of great laudings.
I shall make complaint; and get you many a thwang
    Without another word.
1ST SHEPHERD
Mak, now take out that Southern tooth
    And put in a turd.

MAK
Nay, lads; its only me thou knows,
How goes you; hows the herd?

(*The Mysteries*, 60–1)

3

Remembrance

In an event such as *The Mysteries* where the very oldness of the piece is brought, so to speak, into the present and onto the stage, not as obsolescence but as a 'metre', a lexicon, a performance that still kicks, translation is intimately and fiercely involved in remembrance. Then again, concerns over and processes of remembrance comprehend all of Harrison's written work. So, what might be his latest major lyric, 'The Mother of the Muses' (1990), frames its meditation on memory with a staging of the poet's own efforts at recall – a passage of Aeschylus, of the details of a visit to the memory-impaired inhabitants of a Canadian old people's home, of the war-time bombing of Dresden, and of the signs (mere signs) that testify to what traces remain to us of 'life' and love.[1] In this poem the poet's testament of remembrance works something like the salt-grit sprayer that thaws a passage-way, a means of travelling, through a landscape of frozen memory whose inhabitants – though they may have been the subjects of history (histories in particular of the dislocating travel that was migration) – are iced in now, isolated, with no further journeys to make than the journey towards death:

> And their lives are frozen solid and won't thaw
> with no memory to fling its sparks of salt.

However, the poet's act of testimony, his unfreezing of the dead, is not unproblematic. For a start he never proves able to recall, unaided, the passage of Aeschylus's Greek. The poem concludes with his witnessing, in the snow outside, a bird's tracks, 'like words', 'like blurred Greek', that return to him (and thereby to the reader) the desire for testimony rather than the testimony itself. It is not even the case that memory is returned as through a veil. The bird's tracks are *not* Greek, they are only *like* Cretan Greek to the eye wishing to make the connection, to the intelligence willing to employ the convolutions of simile and metaphor so as to bear witness to the *act* of remembrance, its loving desire. The poet (wittingly) makes a forged connection, with the memories of Harrison's wife's Cretan father, a man who now, in his last days, in Canada, only speaks Greek ('his speech went back, a stowaway, to Crete'), who only speaks the language of his journey's beginning, who appears – unless his daughter and poet son-in-law pick up scraps of the old man's language to throw as sparks of salt into the present scene – to be frozen into a moment of origin.

Fathers and origins (fathers *as* origins): this is familiar Harrisonian ground, as readers of *The School of Eloquence* and *v.* will be able to testify. We would do well, however, to avoid positing a banal conjunction here. For a start (or perhaps, better, for an interim) there is a cautionary pathos in the sort of image that projects the father into the ice of pastness and inarticulacy with a retrospective responsibility, as it were, for teleogy. The *purpose* implied by such teleology would be the poetry of his offspring. The responsibility is too much, and that 'too much' had already been suggested in Harrison's poetry, for example in the quatrain 'Heredity' that heads *The School of Eloquence* in *Selected Poems*:

> How you became a poet's a mystery!
> Wherever did you get your talent from?
> I say: *I had two uncles, Joe and Harry* –
> one was a stammerer, the other dumb.

There, the poet's own vocation, a deliberate endeavour to make eloquent testimony, is staged as a political response to an ineloquent (silent even) precedence. The poem is a response to the unspoken, or not *quite* spoken, demand of ghosts. The 'I say' in the quatrain is not so much an easily-assumed logical connective as an assertion, an in spite of. Heredity is not found in the genes but scratched out upon the blank page, sparks of grit in a whited-out unwritten history. Heredity is an outrageous metaphor, as outrageous as all those painfully 'forged' metaphors ('Each swung cast-iron Enoch of Leeds stress/ clangs a forged music on the frames of Art') by means of which Harrison *forces* one thing to bear relation to another in his poetry. To return to memory, the mother of the muses, that passage of Greek he proves himself unable to recall is a speech from *Prometheus*

Unbound where Prometheus makes claim to having given, in Harrison's précis 'Mankind the gift of writing,/ along with fire the Gods withheld from men'. In Aeschylus's text the skill of writing is linked explicitly to the technology of remembering. From Vellacott's translation:

> Their every act was without knowledge, till I came.
> I taught them to determine when stars rise or set –
> A difficult art. Number, the primary science, I
> invented for them, and how to set down words in writing –
> The all-remembering skill, mother of many arts.[2]

Or, in Paulin's modern adaptation:

> Time and the seasons, the movement of stars and planets, they could measure none of these things. The abstract beauty of pure number, the designing of signs on paper, the infinite accounts in memory banks – they knew nothing of these.[3]

Prometheus's claim is an outrageous presumption, a presumption for which he has been duly punished; and Prometheus's predicament, back there, in mythology, or whatever that scene is where all the lost fathers are restlessly laid, is a pathos. Prometheus had not made the gift of anything that was his own. The fire he gave to mankind was stolen from the gods. Nor did Prometheus bequeath knowledge itself, he bequeathed the technology, the power by means of which knowledge might be exercised: the fire that might fuel the forge in which descriptions, accounts, testimonies might be wrought. The Promethean technology, furthermore, is itself without memory (it is only a technology) unless it suffices to refer to memory as a repetition, a rehearsal, an echo. Harrison stages himself as a Promethean echo, immobile and snowbound into his Toronto domicile just as Prometheus was chained to a rock in the icy mountains, lighting the fire again, attempting that technology:

> After I've lit the fire and looked outside
> and found us snowbound and the roads all blocked,
> anxious to prove my memory's not ossified
> and the way into that storehouse still unlocked

But Harrison finds he has forgotten Prometheus's (Aeschylus's) words. He cannot rehearse them. His memory fails him, although his writing ability is undiminished. It is not, then, a father (or origin)

37

that is recalled. Teresa Stratas's father is not brought back – that gentleman's own utterance is as locked away as Prometheus's speech – but rather a dedication, an acknowledgement is given to him. And we read the '*In memorium*', and maybe we are affected, not because Emmanuel Stratas is given to us (or even memories *of* him), but because we recognize in the poet's desire, exercised through the Promethean technology that is the art of writing, our own desire to play father to our own lost origins: to find written out for us, for instance in someone else's poem, or like birds' tracks in the snow (unintentional signs, as far as our own interests are concerned, of which we feel ourselves the sole diviners), our own intentions, our own loving dedications to the landscapes of our lives.

However, and it is a large 'however', there is an imperative in this poem, as there is in the other major pieces I wish to consider in this chapter, *The School of Eloquence* and *v.*, to make remembering work. The imperative is a political one. If I wrote above of the poet exercising his art to lay out a loving allegiance to parents, and to the histories of 'dispersal and displacement, willed or not' that were lived out by those parents whose own memories are now on the wane, it needs saying that the poem also articulates the necessity of remembering 'horrors to be true'. If one part of Prometheus's gift of fire was the 'gentle' technology that enables the warm articulation of love, the other part was the fire that burns and erases, 'what the *Luftwaffe* unleashed, *and* the Lancaster', burning books but also burning bodies, in Dresden, in the Nazi deathcamps, and, more recently, in the Gulf War (poems in the same 1992 volume, *The Gaze of the Gorgon*, that contains 'The Mother of the Muses' address the Gulf War explicitly). The imperative is political because it is an issue of intervention, of intention, and Harrison states his intention clearly:

> I resolve to bring all yesterday to mind,
> our visit to your father, each fact, *all*.

That '*all*' has to aspire to inclusiveness, and it is something of the nature of that inclusiveness that makes these poems long. Their length is a body of detail, and with the evoking of the detailed body it is perhaps the moment to reference the less conspicuous term in the family romance that seems to inform Harrison's narrative principles: the mother.[4] She is there in the title of the present poem, 'The Mother of the Muses', but then again she is hardly there at all. Or is she? The implied Promethean myth is that the technology of writing and measuring, inherited through fathers and uncles, will serve to bring into relief the feminized body of suffering that *is* memory; and a maternal body in the sense that it will give birth to the political imperatives (you must give remembrance to this pain!) that justify art. Perhaps I infer too much, but there is enough material for my inference in the examples that Harrison quotes (transposed from a TV documentary) of testimonies to the Allied bombing of Dresden during World War II. Eva, a woman Harrison's own age, 'remembers cellar ceiling crashing/ and her mother screaming shrilly: *Swine! Swine! Swine!*' A Dresden zookeeper remembers 'a mother chimp, her charges all dismembered' and, what infers for this reader a hideous unbirthing, 'the gutless gorilla still clutching fruit/ mashed with its bowels into bloody lumps'. Maternal or not, the overt gendering of narrative structure should be familiar enough by now to Harrison's readers, so familiar that we might read as typical that final scenario of the wife, sleeping, her pillow 'still damp from last night's weeping', while

> In that silent dark I swore I'd make it known,
> while the oil of memory feeds the wick of life
> and the flame from it's still constant and still bright,
> that, come oblivion or not, I loved my wife
> in that long thing where we lay with day like night.

That scene, or similar, has been given us in 'Newcastle is Peru' and *v.*, to give just the two most striking examples. My present purpose is not to call Harrison out to answer the charge of practising masculinist poetics, but to note what in fact I regard to be a laudable index of his work, that being what I perceive to be his assertion that memory, history, subject-matter is a material body, of suffering (a history of suffering bodies); but one that might appear to be subject to dematerialization without the perpetual articulation of responsible testimony. So, he refers us in this poem to the likes of Ernst Zundel 'who denies the Jews were gassed', and he even allows that the motive behind such denials might be the 'hope to put back hope in history', but he makes his own refusal of this palliative, exercising the art bequeathed to him by Prometheus (the first Western myth, perhaps, of the body that suffers on behalf of others) to put on record instead the real suffering his own eyes and ears have been witness to.

Even so, these good intentions do not in themselves overcome the difficulties involved in historical recall. The inclusiveness that extends 'The Mother of the Muses' over seven and a half pages of close type is at the service of collating testimony that is either second-hand (that TV documentary) or else, actually, beyond recall (the Alzheimer's-afflicted memory banks of these residents of the Home for the Aged). It is pertinent, too, that the old people he describes, a Ukrainian, a Scot, a Cretan, are immigrants, subjects of translations that seem to have returned in time, in memory, to their source tongues – and even the master-translator Harrison is beyond bringing that material now into the present light. This same historiographical problematic extends throughout the as-yet unfinished sequence *The School of Eloquence*.

To speak of the sequence as unfinished might imply, at a glance, a rhetorical failing. We might recall, for instance, Ezra Pound's great epic, the *Cantos*, which, without resolving itself, revolves (in its closing fragments) a modernist hubris – that would have included so much history, so much mythology, so much wrath within an achieved form – into a staging of its own formal impossibility, a recognition of its own debilitating investment in Fascist politics, and its author's own broken and moving admission:

> And I am not a demigod,
> I cannot make it cohere.
> If love be not in the house there is nothing.
> The voice of famine unheard.[5]

Harrison is probably historically immune to the high modernist hubris that scuppered Pound, and certainly their politics are incommensurable, and Harrison has always happily, it seems, offered his sequence as unfinishing itself, as *continuous*. However, with the structuring of the sequence, as it stands at present, into three sections, and with the insertion of new poems into particular places in the sequence order each time a new edition of *Selected Poems* is published, *The School of Eloquence* (or should we be calling it 'from *The School of Eloquence*'?) offers itself as an *oeuvre* more along the lines of Pound's *Cantos* than, say, the more freewheeling shape of John Berryman's *Dream Songs*. A significant aspect of the comparison is the way that Harrison's sequence perpetually focuses on the persona of its 'maker' (a very Poundian emphasis) so as to stage the issue of the political imperatives contingent upon the poet's assumption of a vocation. I would wish to argue that Harrison offers the poet's vocation in something like the terms outlined above in my discussion of 'The Mother of the Muses'. That is to say, the poet is obliged to educate himself into and utilize the technologies of his craft so as to effect a remembering. 'Each/ rebarbative syllable, remembrancer raise/ 'mob' *rhubarb-rhubarb* to a tribune's speech', declares a passage from the second poem in the sequence, drawing attention to the very materiality of the stuff the poet works with – syllables, phonemes – and promising a raising, through remembrancing, of speech that had been denigrated once as mere sound, into meaning that, now, might have its say in the body politic. To the extent that this is a political-historical project it is, of its nature, unfinishable.

Remembrance, its technologies and its affects, flood the sequence, just as the rising Blackpool tides, like tides of time, like tears that cloud the eye the moment it has apprehended its object, flood the moats of (remembered) sandcastles in 'The Icing Hand', destroying those impermanent little monuments to the maker's art, bringing back, with a gesture that erases the possibility of sustained recall, memories (again) of Harrison's baker father:

> Remembrance like iced cake crumbs in the throat,
> remembrance like windblown Blackpool brine
> overfills this poem's shallow moat
> and first, ebbing, salts, then, flowing, floods this line
>
> (GG 27)

This is a late poem, first published in 1992 (the sequence was begun around 1971, according to Astley's chronology), but its gesture is familiar to readers of the earlier poems of bereavement in Section Two of the sequence.[6] The repetition of mourning here says something about the impossibility of an achieved remembrance, and if there is a formal dialectic to the sequence it lies perhaps in the tension between the completion of the sixteen-line form in each instance, with its symmetrical rhymes, its full pentameters, the punning closure of its metaphors, and the ever-to-be-repeated attempt to 'try shaping memories', as the present poem has it. The body of the memory, or the remembered body, somehow evades the body of the poem.

'The Icing Hand' (the hand that iced the bridal cake, the icy hand of the Grim Reaper – our assumption of Harrison's puns becomes a reflex the more we read), with that final alexandrine that pathetically overextends the pattern of pentameter quatrains, appears perhaps more knowing about the technologies of remembrance than some of the earlier pieces. For example, 'Marked With D.', from the same narrative block (poems which remember Harrison's father in terms of baker's metaphors), is almost triumphant in its metaphoric achievement:

> The baker's man that no one will see rise
> and England made to feel like some dull oaf
> is smoke, enough to sting one person's eyes
> and ash (not unlike flour) for one small loaf.

(*SP* 155)

The technique here is not so much a remembrancing as an appropriation of the baker's body into figures of speech, where those figures of speech seem to claim an achieved resurrection, a transfiguration of the dead man, the lost man, into a metaphoric complex that will suffice, and suffice for some time to come. So, the cremation smoke is 'enough' to perpetuate a mourning effect (to make one person, at least, seem to cry), the ashes 'enough' to knead a metaphoric loaf with that *will* 'rise'. However, the diminutives, the singularities in that verse ('*one* person's eyes', '*one small* loaf'), the negation of the material effect ('no one will see rise'), and the fact that, after all, the poem stages the *desire* to make a tribute that will stand up afterwards (those phrases throughout: 'I thought of', 'I thought how') while narrating the disappearance of the father's body in the crematorium, bring us back to the personal and nontransferable aspects of mourning. It is, after all, Harrison's eyes that get stung and not ours. The metaphoric closure of the poem, after all, speaks of the disappearance of the body that the metaphors would have closed upon.

All of which is fair enough, and affecting enough, for a sequence of poems about personal bereavement. However, I have already asserted that there is a wider political agenda at stake in this sequence, an agenda that is referenced, anyway, in poems such as the above by lines like 'The baker's man that [...] England made to feel like some dull oaf'. To simplify, at the risk of being reductionist, that agenda involves giving voice to the class politics whose oppressive hegemony is articulated in the line 'Some could articulate, while others not' (SP 179). The poem's political task, then, is to be the articulater, remembrancer. 'Wherever hardship held its tongue the job/ 's breaking the silence of the worked-out-gob' (SP 124). And, in this context, the remembrancing of silenced speech into the quasi-permanence of published writing ('black printer's ems/ by which all eloquence gets justified', SP 172) is imperative. If remembrancing is such a slippery task, then the project is problematic.

I want to address this problematic, and then suspend (for want of space) this discussion of the sequence, by considering again later poems, in particular the mini-sequence 'Sonnets for August 1945', only published together at present in The Gaze of the Gorgon. The choice is made partly because other commentators have already written eloquently about the more well-known poems, but also because these particular lyrics extend the issues of political remembrance into new and more comprehensively difficult areas. And, because, having just reread the sequence, and done so in 1995 when the fiftieth anniversaries of VE and VJ will have been commemorated (and celebrated), these eight poems strike this reader as one of Harrison's finest and most moving achievements. And, immediately, I want to turn the discussion away from issues of class, although Harrison himself has given me the cue with his use of the particle '[uz]', that phonetic transcription of the pronoun by which one performs (literally, pronounces) one's allegiance to northern English, working-class communities and histories.

Of course, it would be a betrayal of Harrison's work and, I suspect, the interests of his readers, to sideline the issue of class, and I hope that the present work does not do that. It seems important here, however, in the space available, to portray Harrison as a poet who opens the case of British class conflict into *other* geopolitical areas; *and* – this is just as significant – returns a whole range of concerns that might have been considered extraneous to class politics *back* to class. I elaborate on these ideas in the brief discussion of *The Trackers of Oxyrhyncus*. The real betrayal, after all, would be to bracket class politics as a particular or separate area of concern. It informs and pervades.

To return to the above discussion, to pronounce the word 'us' thus is to buy into an inclusiveness that is also a particular exclusivity, though not an élitist one: a speech community marked by their (our) systematic exclusion from certain authorized modes of participation in discursive practices. The staging of that particle, however, was already, it seems, always opening up a critique of what sort of understandings might be comprehended by the word 'we' – understandings (and misunderstandings) that necessarily extend further than, while including, the issues of English class politics. So, for example, the opening poem of *The School of Eloquence* itself, 'On Not Being Milton', which explicitly narrates, and participates in, class war battles, is dedicated to the literary and social revolutionaries of the Martinique FRELIMO party, and includes within the body of the Poem an allusion to Aimé Césaire's *négritude* classic *Cahier d'un Retour au Pays Natal*.[7] The cue offered here is to infer an extension of the poetry's politics to other areas of cultural antagonism. 'Sonnets for August 1945' actually employs the Leeds working-class community (and 'community' is precisely the right word here) that Harrison grew up in as its *mise-en-scène*, but does so so as to narrate a process of recall ('remembering' given simply is perhaps *not* the right word) that is an education, for the poet-protagonist, into concerns that challenge the values and structures by means of which that community celebrated its 'us'-ness.

The pretext for the sequence is a remembering of VJ Day, Victory in Japan day, the day achieved – according to the general historical wisdom in the West – by the dropping of atomic bombs on Hiroshima and Nagasaki; but the scene of the sequence, at first, is a celebration of that event. The opening poem of the mini-sequence remembers a VJ street party. The poem's title, 'The Morning After, I' implies an immediate recall, and indeed the scene describes the morning-after marks of the celebration bonfire, 'The fire left to itself might smoulder weeks'. Of course, the recall is actually something like fifty years after the event, and that distance allows Harrison a nostalgia for a form of community celebration, an us-ness, that 'has never come again since as a boy / I saw Leeds people dance and heard them sing'. Even over such a distance of time, though, the bonfire's mark is still visible, 'There's still that dark, scorched circle on the road'. Still burning? The assertion of memory in that line is a political moment because, of course, the burning that really needs to be referenced is the incineration that took place in Japan; and, as we

44

look back over the poem, we find that horror implied in the apparent excess of the images that seemed, at first, only to be describing the Leeds street-scene: 'Phone cables melt. Paint peels from off back gates. Kitchen windows crack'.[8] If we make that recognition then we might hear the poem's title to be punning on the phrase 'the *mourning* after' (mourning for others), a paradox in a poem about celebration (celebrating ourselves), and a paradox that the poem refuses to make explicit at the level of its declarations. Even the phrase 'VJ' is not footnoted, we have to look it up in our history books, or else already know what it implies. Like the grief that might swell out of mourning, the realization that might only dawn in the hangover of the morning after, the possibility of a politicized remembering oozes through the poem's images like an unconscious; and the poems that follow rehearse a process of bringing that unconscious into the light. So, brilliantly (literally), the second piece, 'The Mornng After, II', illumines the darkening of those Japanese cities in 1945. 'The Rising Sun was blackened on those flames.' The scene is of a burning of the Japanese flag at that same previous day's party, by unremembering boys for whom 'Hiroshima, Nagasaki were mere names'; but the recall of the scene, now, made by one of those same boys (Harrison) allows a politicized understanding to begin to be heard. We hear those British Empire 'Rule Britannias' that informed the community's celebration of itself; and we hear, in the phrase 'jabbering tongues', that racist othering which is the other face of the same red-hot coin. The poem returns in its final quatrain to the bonfire's scorched circle, but sees in it now

> a night-sky globe nerve-wrackingly all black,
> both hemispheres entire but with no stars,
> an Archerless zilch, a Scaleless zodiac.

(GG 10)

We might remember that involved in the Promethean gift of the technologies of recording and remembering was the measuring of 'the movement of stars and planets', but it appears now that Prometheus's other gift of destroying fire has erased those signs. Memory, then, politicized remembering, cannot afford to be dependent on the ready availability of signs (this has always been Harrison's theme, as bard of the silenced and buried subjects of suppressed histories). Or else, it must reread the available signs,

45

and find more (or less) than the signs appear to offer, as does the next poem, 'Old Soldier', meditating upon the label of the CAMP Coffee extract bottle (it showed a Sikh servant waiting upon a kilted soldier of the British Raj), seeing, in the light of the A-bomb attacks, a mere reduplication and hollowing of British Empire icons, 'a last chuprassie with all essence gone'.

The story is a story of the necessary loss of innocence; even a self-schooling into such loss (perhaps *that* is the school of eloquence). This is an education that is revisited in the next three poems through the idea of the photograph – or, more properly, the 'Snap' (title of the sixth poem): the snap in 'that fraying Kirby wire' of innocence that might have held one, grinning, between the pages of the family album,

> that briefly held the whole weight of the nation
> over the common element of fire
> that bonded the A-bomb blast to celebration
>
> (GG 14)

and, in our own recent history, has held the liberal demagogue to the sufficiency of a slogan: 'Ban the Bomb!' Harrison's intellectual scepticism is too practised to suffer such slogans as an adequate response to the dilemmas posed by the atomic explosions.[9] In the same fashion he finds himself forced to see, in loved mementos of a loving family ('I've never seen a family group so glad/ of its brief freedom, so glad to be alive'), a 'figure' in the frame that seems to send the family towards the photographer, 'the biped dressed in black', the freezer of the moment, as if towards death. Innocence is compromised *in the recall*, by knowledge acquired after the event. The snap of a 'happy and pre-teen' Harrison in 1945, playing 'the part of innocence', is an image that never could have been because we did not have, then, the cheap Japanese cameras we have now. And that 'innocence' is, knowing what we know now, an 'innocence that never could have been'. If one were to recall the innocence of a pre-Hiroshima Peter Pan, the boy who would not grow up, one would 'have to keep returning to Japan/ till the blast-cast shape walks with him off the wall'. But to keep returning, to a place one has yet to visit, is hardly to return once and for all: that innocence (of death) is a fictive romance, now, and our attempts to capture it, say in photography, serve an opposite function – the click of the camera sounds like the ticking of Captain Hook's clock in the belly of the crocodile that has a taste

46

for our blood. We hear the shutter click and, as in Harrison's earlier sonnet 'Study', our minds move upon silence and the visit to Hades of the *Aeneid*, Book VI:

> Now everything gets clicked at the loud clock
> the shots and shutters sound like's Captain Hook's
> ticking implacably inside the croc.
>
> (GG 13)

SMEE (*sombrely*). Some day the clock will run down, and then he'll get you.

HOOK (*a broken man*). Ay, that is the fear that haunts me.[10]

So, in the seventh poem, 'First Aid in English', Harrison goes back to school, to his first grammar book, to fail to find there collective nouns for the acts of collectivized murder (ghulag, ghetto, genocide, atomic blast) that have scarred twentieth-century world history even more indelibly than the 1945 victory bonfire scarred 'that dark, scorched circle on the [Leeds] road'. Such a finding, such a naming and acknowledgement, anyway, would only at best be a mere patching up, a 'first aid'. As the last poem in the sequence, 'The Birds of Japan', has it, if the birds cremated above the blast had a last song to sing, that song never descended on any 'Bomb-Age Basho, or a Hokusai'. Although remembrance is a political imperative, Harrison can only, at last, testify to the imperative itself, ironically juxtaposing the singing of the VJ celebrations against his own, necessarily, unfinished song:

> Apostles of that pinioned Pentecost
> of chirrupings cremated on the wing
> will have to talk their ghosts down, or we're lost.
> Until we know what they sang, who can sing?
>
> (GG 16)

I've spoken of remembrance as a 'political imperative', but perhaps now I need to take a cue from Harrison's technique and question the facile assumption of a phrase that, in the course of writing this chapter, has become a reflex: as reflex as the aerosolling of 'UNITED' over the gravestones of a Beeston cemetery just up the road from Leeds United's Elland Road football ground. A word, a phrase, spattered over mementos to the dead. In the scene narrated in the poem *v.*, Harrison himself comes across this graffito (he is here to pay fleeting respect to his parents' grave)

47

and his response is to want to erase what has been lazily, and clumsily, sprayed over the chiselled inscriptions – if only he had time in his busy life to do that. *Or else* (and here's the rub, at least the poet's alternative to rubbing away the commentaries that will, anyway, accrue) re-inscribe those commentaries, here in his poem, with a meaning born out of his own desire: 'I know/ what the UNITED that the skin sprayed *has* to mean'. He claims an imperative backed by certainty ('I know': I must) but in fact what he knows is that the imperative is predicated not by knowledge but by desire, and maybe a frustrated desire at that: certainly a desire no more or less valid (how might such validity be measured anyway?) than the frustrated desires of the dole-wallah skinhead who sprayed the desecration in the first place. Anyway, he himself could have been that desecrator, that skinhead is his own *alter ego* ('He aerosolled his name. And it was mine'). So, while Harrison the mature poet extrapolates from the graffito a hymn to love and marriage in his verses, his sceptical Other ('a voice that scorns chorales is yelling: Wanker!') chants the facts-of-like antagonisms in these UNITED 'versuses'. The one banks upon the other. Both bank upon desire:

> My *alter ego* wouldn't want to know it,
> his aerosoll vocab would balk at LOVE,
> the skin's UNITED underwrites the poet,
> the measures carved below the ones above.

(SP 248)

And what does desire bank upon? Like the graves banked up on Beeston Hill, overlooking a vista of Leeds city (there is a reproduction of the view on the cover of *Selected Poems*), and poised above the hollow darkness of a worked-out coalpit, the desires of skinhead and poet are invested in temporality, in shares of futurity or oblivion. Here is where the politics of remembrance return, with this return in the present tense to the remembered Leeds scene and the binary antagonisms of *Loiners* and *The School of Eloquence*, with a shift this time between the idealism of remembrance and the pragmatics of desire:

> Hindu/Sikh, soul/body, heart v. mind,
> East/West, male/female, and the ground
> these fixtures are fought out on's Man, resigned
> to hope from his future what his past never found.

(SP 238)

The refrain of the poem, codifying that desire, is the 'la-la *Lohengrin*' of the familiar bridal march, 'Here Comes the Bride'. We hear – or rather Harrison hears, or desires to hear – this populist appropriation of Wagner's operatic march four times during the course of the monologue; the first time as five kids hum it as a joke, banging their football against a hawthorn tree to make the mayblossom fall, and finally (in the ear of the poet's desire) as 'ghosts from all Leeds matches humming/ with one concerted voice the bride, the bride'. All the Leeds United skinheads ever join in the hymn to Harrison's own personal locus of love, 'the bride/ I feel united to, *my* bride'. I used to balk at this bit of the poem, it all seemed a bit too marital basically, a reduction of complex antagonisms to a spuriously essentialist and cosy heterosexism. Now, though, it seems as if the poem even invites such objections, but faces them off while acknowledging that the values, the imperatives that the poem espouses are traced out over a 'worked-out seam' that may cave in any day.[11] It is as if Harrison offers his own poem, with its 'CUNT, PISS, SHIT and (mostly) FUCK!' as an expletive, as a graffito sprayed over dark times (one tends to refer to 'the Thatcher years'). His love-song, like the skin's peeved ejaculations, like the 'brief chisellable bits' on the gravestones, is thrown to the future as a hostage to remembrance. This is the tone with which the poem begins and ends, from 'Next millennium you'll have to look quite hard' to the final epitaph offered up to the yet-unborn 'poetry-supporter'. Not testimony so much as testament, like the similarly belligerent testament of W. B. Yeats's 'Under Ben Bulben' (though again, as with the Pound comparison above, the politics are ostensibly poles apart from Harrison's). There is, in the end (which of course is *not* an end if the earth and the people on it continue to effect those magical recycling processes 'that hew the body's seams to get the soul') nothing to remember, other than what we choose to remember, 'choose to love' and value. The poem reminds us '*how poems can grow from* (beat you to it) SHIT'. That may be how, even as our memories fail us, remembrance works: '*look behind*'. Looking, however, and being looked at (or more pertinently *not* being looked at) is a problem again. It is even a terror. The final chapter will follow Harrison's open-eyed pursuit of the terrorizing gaze of the Gorgon.

4

The Poet and the Gorgon

The gaze of the Gorgon, the title of Harrison's 1992 BBC film/ poem and the eponymous image of his volume of poems for that year, which was his first book-length collection for over a decade, presides over much of his later work. The image recalls earlier presiding influences, the gargoyle of 'Prague Spring', about to puke his wassail on the listening throng that will appear for the morrow's Mayday military parade; or the stone head of the satyr on the cover of *U.S. Martial*, tuned into the New York chatter, presiding over the poet's transmission of Martial's Roman epigrams into a contemporary urban vernacular. In both those earlier examples the poet simultaneously sets himself apart from the stone head, while allying himself with its presiding vantage – and that vantage is the sort of cultural supervision he stages himself as occupying in other instances, for example when he describes his role in *The Mysteries* as the 'Yorkshire poet who came to read the metre'. Although the Gorgon's gaze offers a significant twist on those earlier images – importantly, the Gorgon's incorporation of terror for and hatred of humanity means that hers is an influence that must be *opposed* by the poet – we will miss something of the specific *mise-en-scène* of Harrison's poetic if we ignore the extent to which the poet takes on for himself the vantage of the presiding gaze, even if that be the gaze of the Gorgon. For him the presiding vantage is to do with seeing, knowing and speaking on behalf of. But with the Gorgon we are into opposite areas, of *non*-seeing (those eyeless faces of the warrior Achilles' helmet and the Gulf War tank that adorn the cover of *The Gaze of the Gorgon*); the erasure of memory and understanding, and the obliteration of speech (the *Gorgon* film includes a hideous montage of war-shattered faces: 'What poems will this mouth recite?'). That is to say, the vantage that the poet would occupy (recalling his earlier combative use of that word: 'We'll occupy your lousy leasehold poetry') is one that, in terms of the present myth, threatens the technologies and values that he would espouse. There is a sense here in which poetry is encountering, through displacement, its own fear of itself. The gaze of the Gorgon Medusa, which turns to stone those that meet its gaze with their own gaze, was, I remember, one of the more frightening myths I absorbed in childhood. But perhaps it would be: it is a myth of castration – if only for the heterosexual male – though we were reassured that that fate was returned, so to speak, upon the Gorgon when the hero Perseus averted *his* gaze, caught Medusa's reflection in his shield and decapitated the snake-headed female monster. And, of course, the Gorgon is still a castrating monster in Harrison's work: that point is made explicit in 'A Cold Coming' with the poem's reiterated focus upon war's threat to the (male) body's procreative function. And yes, as the epigraph to *Selected Poems* reminds us ('... *son io il poeta/essa la poesia*), this *is* a masculinist poetic, the threat to poetic utterance *is* analogous to castration, but we need to say also that the image is more extensive than that. We might suggest that the Gorgon is the war-god (the 'Geldshark') Ares as often as it is Medusa, or at least the stare of Ares' son Phobos – born to Ares of the love goddess Cytherea (Aphrodite) – stamped, according to Hesiod, into the shield of the brutalist hero Heracles.[1] Certainly throughout Harrison's writing the Gorgon's henchmen are hench*men*. *The Blasphemers' Banquet* (the July 1989 BBC film/poem that responded to the still-unresolved Salman Rushdie affair)[2] and *The Gaze of the Gorgon* line up the culprits: Kaiser Wilhelm II, Hitler, Stalin, the Ayatollah Khomeini and so on. The Gorgon's curse is a murdering *machismo* and, in Harrison's sexualized schema, it is women (the Greenham Common protesters of *The Common Chorus*, Hecuba at the fall of Troy who haunts all of Harrison's later theatre work, the female munitionettes and performers of *Square Rounds*) or else the feminized poet (the rowdy squaddy of 'The Act', in *The Gaze of the Gorgon* would 'brand the [poet] freak as "queer"') who are given the role of countering that macho, supremacist curse. However, such gendered and sexualized inversions, taking into account the extent to which Harrison comes down so often in favour of the heterosexual marriage as *the* touchstone of value and continuity,

51

involve the poet and his readers in a schema which is not without its theoretical difficulty.

That is to say, there is an idea lodged in that schema, in which the poet sides with the women *outside* the missile silos while finding words for the sexual abuse visited upon them by the soldiers across the wire; or in which he stages his own feminization by the macho squaddies getting pissed on the Belfast–Newcastle flight, which develops what might have been either a banal myth of castration or else a banally appropriative male 'feminism' to say something more interesting about art's complicity in the terrors it combats. That idea has something to do with the critiques of Apollonian high-art culture palaces in *Gorgon* and the National Theatre version of *Trackers*, those places where Harrison's own work is or might be staged. It has something to do with the argument over versification in the early scenes of the October 1992 National Theatre play *Square Rounds*, where the scientists who develop modern chemical warfare (themselves caught in a Catch-22 complicity of inventing technologies for humanity's survival that simultaneously function as technologies of mass-destruction) pride themselves on their ability to rhyme. It has to do also, I feel, with the montage techniques of the *Gorgon* film, where the century's victims are frozen out of colour footage into black and white stills, or the narrative technique of *Trackers* where the satyrs are frozen – as both yobs and victims – into icons of their own dispossession, inside a historical unknowing, as it were, which the poet-dramatist, the poet *behind* all this, with full 20-20 vision, presides over: seeing and pitying.

The problem has something to do with pity itself, an emotion that the poet Yeats, excluding Wilfrid Owen's war poems from his *Oxford Book of Modern Verse*, insisted had no proper place in poetry.[3] It is precisely pity, however, that distinguishes the presiding vantage occupied by the poet from the *same* vantage occupied by the Gorgon, although both – as we shall see – are figures of stone. An earlier poet-dramatist caught at the issue thus:

> *Enter Lear with Cordelia in his arms.*
> LEAR. Howl, howl, howl, howl! O, you are men of stones:
> Had I your tongues and eyes, I'd use them so
> That heaven's vault should crack. She's gone for ever!
> She's dead as earth. Lend me a looking-glass;

Why, then she lives.
KENT.   Is this the promised end?
EDGAR.   Or image of that horror?

(Shakespeare, *King Lear*, V.3)

Lear brings the evidence, the human victim, the detritus of war, onto the stage to be seen, and if such things are looked upon how can one not pity? But Lear's own pity is either an imageless howl, or else an incapacity to *see* what is in his own arms for what he knows it to be: his daughter dead. Between the horror and the image of that horror, pity's gob is stopped: *or else* pity speaks, speaks that 'image', and speaks that image into a being (*as* image) it did not have, could not have in the incomprehensible non-being of death, real death. The defining image in Harrison's later work for what I am trying to articulate here is the stone memorial to Heinrich Heine, perpetually displaced across the narrative of *Gorgon*. The dissident nineteenth-century German-Jewish poet Heine is petrified, literally. He is a man of stone. He cannot see, he cannot speak, but Harrison gives him words to speak what he might have seen (pitiful images we do see in the film of the poem) but to speak also of the poet's own frustrating disarmament, his failure, his castration if you like, his 'presiding' over the pitiful misappropriation of human resources:

> I can do nothing, even cry.
> Tears are for the living eye.
> So weep, you still alive to shed
> the tears I can't shed, being dead.
> And if I could I'd shed my tears
> that in the century's closing years
> the nation's greatest souls preside
> over such spirit-suicide,
> and that in 1992
> Schiller, Goethe, Heine view
> the new banks rising by the hour

(GG 63)

The poem concludes with the proposal that 'to keep new Europe open-eyed/ they let the marble poet preside...'. There are paradoxes there, then, of seeing and not-seeing, of speaking and not being heard, of pursuing a political imperative and being unable to act. It is the idea of being turned to stone, and this is a petrification not unlike that of the frozen semen of the American marines 'A Cold Coming': at the same time a hubristic bid for posterity and an implicit acknowledgement of the idea – and what more, for the living, can it be than an 'idea'? – of mortality. Heine, in Harrison's version, is a more benevolent presiding genius than the gargoyle of 'Prague Spring' or the satyr head of *U. S. Martial* or, of course, the Gorgon herself, and Harrison borrows this benevolence to characterize his own work. Fair enough, that benevolence, and that pity, are there on his page. But swastikas are daubed on Heine's stone face, junkies' blood is caught in his stone hair. In the blindness of the petrified poet who reflects upon that which he does not see, who catches the Gorgon's image in the mirror-shield of his own images, there is a sense in which he catches and gives back, that is to say *stages*, the terrors he wields his pen against.

That sense, I want to argue, is a sense of theatre, and in this final chapter I intend to develop these ideas into a consideration of Harrison's particular forms of theatricality. But first we need to return to the stone, the memorial. The idea of being turned to stone still haunts. What haunts that idea, I suspect, is the notion of haunting one's own death; of being petrified *inside* one's own memorial. If existential death, unbeing, is something that we cannot know for ourselves, or even know about – something that we can only frame with the discourse of the living, and therefore still not know *as such* – the idea of being turned to stone still just manages to catch at the limit, the border (the border between the living and the petrified flesh) of what we can conceive of our own death. And the terror that we conceive at that border, to know and to say 'our own death', is the terror of not, in fact, being able to *say* anything at all.[4] This terror is peculiar to poets. Or rather, to conceive of the terror in such terms is to conceive the conditions and limits for poetry and, unsurprisingly, poets have meditated eloquently on that frozen mouth. More interestingly, though, especially in the context of the present discussion, some of the most resonant of those meditations have been made by poets who have expended the majority of their energies in the theatre – or at least in words written to be spoken. I am thinking, for example, as I often do, of the Irish poet-dramatist W. B. Yeats, who in poems like 'A Dialogue of Self and Soul' and 'Vacillation' *refuses* the absolute, transcendental knowledge of the Soul in everlasting Heaven, in favour of the partial, messy ignorance of the living Self in the world. Hence:

> Only the dead can be forgiven;
> But when I think of that my tongue's a stone.

Hence:

> *The Soul.* Seek out reality, leave things that seem.
> *The Heart.* What, be a singer born and lack a theme?
> *The Soul.* Isaiah's coal, what more can man desire?
> *The Heart.* Struck dumb in the simplicity of fire!
> *The Soul.* Look on that fire, salvation walks within.
> *The Heart.* What theme had Homer but original sin?

A chilling motif for such meditations, at least in modern literature in English, might be the last phrase Shakespeare gives to the dying Hamlet, 'the rest is silence', that moment just after the one in which the Prince bequeaths his inheritance to Fortinbras with the uncanny words 'he has my dying voice'. That utterance, that vote, was Hamlet's last contribution to the political situation; it was his attempt to ensure that the situation continued, less violently, after his own passing. It was an optimistic input into political contingency. But whatever it is that Hamlet *knows*, a knowledge that we too, when we read or watch the play, feel we have had a glimpse at – just as in *Lear* we somehow perceive the 'horror' that on stage is only an 'image of that horror' – is carried in silence to the grave. Fortinbras, the late-comer, the inheritor, knows nothing. He, arriving at the play's conclusion, promises that Hamlet will be memorialized ('for his passage/ The soldiers' music and the rites of war/Speak loudly for him') but in militaristic terms that don't seem to quite do justice to the Hamlet in whose company we have spent the last four hours. Fortinbras himself seems to recognize this slip as he surveys the dead bodies: 'Such a sight as this,/ Becomes the field, but here shows much amiss', and we might be inclined to gloss his observation with the comment that it is precisely such a detail as the 'soldiers shoot' at the play's last line that petrifies the poetry – the pity – that might have been spoken for these bodies. We feel we know this, but it is not said.

The modern German poet-dramatist Heiner Müller suggests an inflection on all this, concluding a play of his that uses the Greek story of Medea and Jason to stage the terrors and atrocities of colonialism with the lines:

The theatre of my death
was opened for business as I stood among the mountains
in the circle of dead companions on the stone
And the expected aeroplane appeared above me
Without having to think I knew
that this machine was what
my grandmothers had given the name God
The airblast swept the corpses off the plateau
and shots slammed into my tottering flight
I felt MY blood leaking out of MY veins
and MY body translating into the landscape
of MY death
        IN THE BACK THE BASTARDS
The rest is poetry
            Who has the better teeth
the blood or the stone[5]

'Der Rest ist Lyrik', but we might read Müller's phrase as sardonic. The rest is mere poetry, it will not capture the transcendental suffering of MY death, nor will it redeem the horror of all those other sufferings that my death images and, eventually, joins in silence. Tony Harrison, in work such as the film/poem *The Gaze of the Gorgon*, has words and images that enable us to feel the bite of both the blood of the century's murdered *and* the memorializing stone. And, at the risk of putting words into a poet's mouth (Harrison has words enough of his own, but he himself does not balk at ventriloquizing Heinrich Heine) we might suggest that Harrison's inflection on Hamlet's dying words would be 'the rest *has to be* poetry'. It has to be, because to speak against the Gorgon's petrifying gaze is not only to sing the stretch of the sensuous self (though that too is important, as is made clear for example in *The Blasphemers' Banquet's* Khayyamic refrain 'I love this fleeting life'), but to speak also against those blasphemous scars upon the century's corpse that were 'gulag, ghetto, genocide'; that have recently been reopened by Operation Desert Shield (not to mention more recent events in Rwanda and the former Yugoslavia); and have hardly yet been negotiated for good by the phallic, mirror-shielded banks ('that reach so high/into the modern Frankfurt sky') being erected over 1990s ECU-land. In fact, those phallic banks, analogous maybe to the art of lyric poetry, image poetry's difficult complicity, comprehending simultaneously the Gorgon's gaze and the shield of the Gorgon-slayer:

> like Gorgon's eyes
> or polished shield of one who slays
> the Gorgon, but can't kill her gaze.

The gaze survives poetry's swipe. These banks too are the places where the money is made that pays for the tickets in the nearby opera house, but art in itself is not immune to the Gorgon's influence:

> Escape, they're thinking, but alas
> that's the Gorgon in the glass.

If the rest has to be poetry, but if poetry itself presides over terror, reflecting terror to us in the mediated form of its images, its *reflections*, then how is the poet's art to be responsibly staged in our time? As Harrison says, in the voice of Heine:

> If art can't cope
> it's just another form of dope,
> and leaves the Gorgon in control
> of all the freedoms of the soul.

How, we are driven to ask, does Harrison's art 'cope'?

The answer has already, in part, been given. Harrison ventriloquizes the petrified stone. Shakespeare's Hamlet was useful to me above, but Harrison's own motif for these considerations is Euripides' Hecuba in *The Trojan Women*. Euripides stages the immediate aftermath of the sacking and destruction of Troy. The Trojan heroes have been slaughtered, the boy-prince Astyanax is murdered in the course of the play, and the Trojan women, about to be shipped into slavery, face a situation for which there is no help. The play, like Cordelia's corpse, is a laceration of our desires to redeem the times by looking *at* them. In his essay 'Hecuba to Us' which prefaces his Greenham-Common-based version of Aristophanes' *Lysistrata*, *The Common Chorus*, Harrison remarks that

> it is left to the one who could be said to have lost most to seek for one last redeeming idea. Hecuba says:

> And yet had not the very hand
> of God gripped and crushed this city deep in the ground,
> we should have disappeared in darkness, and not given
> a theme for music, and the songs of men to come.

57

If we hadn't suffered we wouldn't be songs for 'later mortals'. The song for later mortals is the tragedy being performed. Hecuba addresses the Athenian audience of 415 BC across time from an already mythical and long-ruined Troy. They are the very 'later mortals' whose songs are Hecuba's redemption. Every time the play is played through history in all its versions the 'mortals' become 'later'. [...] We are the latest mortals who guarantee that the suffering was not in vain, and that the chain of commemorative empathy is unbroken.[6]

We find these ideas elaborated on in his 1988 'Presidential Address to the Classical Association', where he counters Sartre's suggestion that Euripides' play ends with 'total nihilism'.[7] Harrison points to Hecuba's first words in the play as she rises from the ground, *ana, dysdaimon* ('Rise, stricken head', in Lattimore's version), and her last word *biou* (life, as in 'the slave's life') as she again rises from the ground so as to exit to an old age of bitterness. He reminds us that the Greek tragic mask, open-eyed, open-mouthed, is precisely *raised*, and raised into the face of the audience, at these desperate moments. As in the 1992 essay, the issue is all in what the mask puts over to the live audience of later mortals:

My dramatic instincts tell me that Euripides brings his Trojan Women low to the ground not only to take a last leave of their dead, but in order that they again had to raise their heads like Hecuba at the beginning of the play, and stand, in order to make an exit. And the bearing of that exit and the deportment of the mask are reasons why we are able to gaze on the terror and not turn to stone.[8]

Further, it is vital to Harrison that the Greek mask is obliged to speak. In this same essay he remembers Hesiod's image of the fifth age of mankind, the age of Iron, when 'Zeus will destroy this race of mortal men [*meropon anthropon*, literally "men gifted with speech"] when they come to have grey hair on the temples at their birth'.[9] He remembers, in our own age, 'babies born literally with their hair already grey in Japan as a result of the A-bombs dropped on Hiroshima and Nagasaki'. He remembers Macneile Dixon's comment from 1921 that tragedy 'must deal with the most monstrous and appalling that life can offer when it turns upon us its Medusa-like countenance of frenzy and despair'. But he remembers too Robert Jay Lifton who, charting

the effect of the Nazi concentration camps and the nuclear holocaust on our imaginations, and the deeply numbing effect of what must be the most petrifying Medusa-like gaze of all on our sense of futurity has called for artists to discover 'a theatre that can imagine the end of the world and go beyond that... [a theatre] that can believe in tomorrow', what he later has to call 'a theatre of faith'. It sounds to me like a call for the *rebirth* of tragedy.

It is the Greek tragic mask, open-eyed, 'designed with an open mouth', that offers a model for that tragic rebirthing, that faces up, literally, to disaster:

> If a mask gazes on the same horrors, the same terrors, it goes on gazing. It is created with open eyes. It has to keep on looking. It faces up to the Muses. What does a mask do when it suffers or witnesses suffering through continually open eyes? Words never fail it. It goes on speaking. It's created with an open mouth. To go on speaking. It has faith in the word.

The presiding gaze and the redeeming idea of the word are brought together in the mask. However, the mask does not speak, not quite. The actor speaks behind and through the mask, and the actor speaks the words given to them by the poet. We are back with the issue of translation and adaptation, which was never an issue simply of shifting a speech into one's own language, but of reoccupying, renegotiating a speech for the demands of the present moment: for these actual later mortals who will listen to this now, on this day, in this theatre. The mask itself is petrified, like the marble poet who might preside over the new Europe, and needs to be perpetually reanimated by actors speaking words of poets. There are at least four agents in the equation: the mask (the mask has a name, 'Hecuba' for instance), the actor, the poet, and the audience of later mortals. The art 'copes' to the extent that it engages that equation in a shared gaze that is neither crippling nor evasive, and I want to conclude this book by considering two examples, one from film and one for the stage, of Harrison's contribution to the perpetuation of Hecuba's example.

The film is *Black Daisies for the Bride* (broadcast by BBC2 on 30 June 1993). Unlike other films made in collaboration with the director Peter Symes and the composer Dominic Muldowney, Harrison does not appear in or speak the text for this piece. *Black Daisies* is made up of footage of a group of residents (all women) on the Alzheimer's ward of High Royds Hospital in Menston.

59

This footage is interspersed with 'fictional' episodes where actresses (who are given, on the first level, to be impersonating staff at High Royds) deliver songs, written by Harrison, which are to be taken as wedding-day memories belonging specifically to the old women we see in the location footage. These songs use the verse-forms of old Tin Pan Alley tunes like 'Daisy, Daisy', and 'Oh! You Beautiful Doll', or the carol 'In the Bleak Midwinter', which are tunes and rhythms that Maria Tobin, Kathleen Dickenson and Muriel Prior *might* remember if, terminally memory-impaired as they are by the tragic condition of Alzheimer's, they remember anything at all.

My use of the present tense to speak of the women themselves is already disingenuous. We are told, for instance, during the film that 'In a few more weeks, though, Muriel Prior dies'.[10] We already know that Alzheimer's is a terminal condition, and we are given to understand also, as we watch the film, that we are watching people who are already, or soon will be, dead. This particular pathos is exacerbated by the fact that what we are watching is a *film*. These people there on the screen actually lived the moments we are seeing, they are not, at least in the raw footage, dramatic 'characters', nor even is their behaviour staged for the camera. This is brought over, paradoxically perhaps, in a touching moment when Kathleen Dickenson appears to recognize and dance to 'Oh! You Beautiful Doll' played by the hospital entertainer. It seems as if she is indeed 'glad she's Kath and alive', as the song Harrison writes for her unremembered younger self has it. However, all this film footage, in the context of the narrative's focus upon the Alzheimer's condition, presents these women to us as masks. The medium of film preserved, it captured, as film (unlike theatrical representation) does, their very ephemerality by representing their materiality; but it captured the women at a moment when – too far gone to Alzheimer's – there was little or no possible retrieving of their memories and experiences. In a televised discussion broadcast the same night of the film, Harrison spoke of hours spent with these women during the filming.[11] He makes remarks to the effect that the women appeared, clearly, to be wanting to communicate *something*, to make proper contact with another human being, even if the substance of their communication was lost. It is as if Alzheimer's, and the medium of film itself, froze these women within a repertoire of performative gestures (Muriel's repeated phrase 'I love you, I love you', Maria's one note from an aria retained from her singing days, Kathleen's obsessive spring-cleaning). Without disrespect to these women, I think these frozen performative gestures are something related to what Harrison means when he speaks in the comments quoted above of the Greek mask. The mask is not neutral, it is not abstract. Like 'Hecuba', the mask testifies to an actual, particular circumstance; but the mask does not (if substantive communication *is* the issue) bring its memories with it. It is up to us, Harrison seems to be saying, at least it is up to poets, to remember on behalf of the mask, to restore its first person in the *present* tense, and this is precisely what Harrison does here in the 'Bridal Songs' that intersperse the finished film.

It could be argued, and Michael Ignatieff makes the suggestion to Harrison's face in the televised discussion, that there is a sentimentality, a presumption here. How can Harrison, or anyone, know what these women *would* remember? Something of that sentimentality comes across in the *gestus* of montage that makes the actual Muriel Prior appear to respond to the fictional younger self who addresses her, back across the future, as it were:

> Muriel! Muriel! My voice in your ear grows less,
> fading into the storm of forgetfulness.
> If life gave back tomorrow
> our memories, joy and sorrow,
> not just the best, but all the rest,
> would you want to relive them...?
>
> MURIEL PRIOR (*The resident in Whernside Ward*)
> ...YES!

(*BD* 25)

Charges of sentimentality aside, we might more pertinently suggest that *actual* memory impairing diseases provide too neat a structural gift for modern dramatists such as Harold Pinter (*A Kind of Alaska*), Peter Brook (*The Man Who...*) or Tony Harrison. Such dramas do lay bare some of the deep-structural bones of a modern theatrical paradigm, the memory play (one could produce a large list that mapped out modernist theatrical achievement just in the terms of this paradigm, naming Ibsen, Strindberg, Yeats, Beckett, Williams, Kantor, Pinter, and Friel for starters). To the extent to which such dramas activate certain narrative structures of repression, recall and recognition they are moving to encounter, and I have certainly been 'touched' by the three mentioned above. However, recalling the messy *difficulty* of *King Lear* or *The Trojan Women* or, to follow Harrison's example and recall an example from (my own) 'real life', of observing a dying parent's brave but painful work of sustaining the threads of a memory under attack from a caustic disease – I am inclined to suggest that the very *achievement* in these works (in terms of drama, staging and poetry), the extent to which these poet-dramatists *do* redeem these historical instances of suffering (and do so, I should add, with a benevolent pity that should not be called exploitative) compromises, after all, the frustration and hatred, the 'howl' that is in the situation also. So, to return specifically to *Black Daisies*, might it not be suggested that the film appears to be too satisfied with the fortuitous adequacy, the readability of its images of confetti-filled blizzards, black daisies for the bride, and marriage-days as the loci *sine qua non* from which self-identity might be recalled?

I should say, while I am in the mood, that I have my problems also with *The Trackers of Oxyrhyncus*, Harrison's play that was performed in a one-off production at the Ancient Stadium at Delphi, Greece, in 1988, and subsequently rewritten for a run at the Royal National Theatre in London and performances at Salt's Mill in Yorkshire and at Art Carnuntum near Vienna. Those ghetto-blasters, for example, that are fobbed off on the satyrs by Apollo, as a sop to their dispossession from Apollonian high art and (more importantly) the significant social agency and privilege of which such high art is a perk, seem a bit of a cheap shot. The image hints at the sort of fogeyish denigration of the urban vernaculars of pop music (and some of the modes of its dissemination *as* popular) that Harrison might once have balked at. Then again, the image also serves to articulate more vital concerns about, for instance, the alienating commercial structures within which popular culture can be handed back down to the populace as a phony, and patronized privilege. And, if this paragraph is shaping up as the space in which I put the same boot into Harrison as the satyrs (picking upon the wrong object for their frustration) put into their leader Silenus, then it should also be the space where this critic expresses a partiality and distances himself from those journals that rather gleefully, it seems, took the opportunity to put the boot into *Square Rounds* on the grounds that there the poet was insulting their intelligence. These were largely the same shrilly conservative organs that had tried to do down Richard Eyre's television film of *v.*, an instance where, if intelligence was the stakes, the measured quatrains left the bold-type headlines screaming in a gale of their own making.[12]

The problem really worth addressing here (and all right, it is a problem which *Square Rounds* does partake of) is one Harrison addresses himself, through another 'presiding' persona, in the poem 'The Pomegranates of Patmos'. Here, a character from 2,000 years ago presides over a man and wife walking the Patmos beach in the present day ('I follow them lovingly strolling'). This is one of Harrison's benevolent vantages, looking so as to see clearly, dedicating a speech 'not [to] the hereafter, [but] the *here*'. The character remembers his/her brother Prochorus aiding St John's composition of the Apocalyptic Book of Revelations and contributing to that text's fantastic anticipation of Armageddon a specifically poetic technique. This is a technique that enables the appropriation of any available material substance into metaphors that feed a closed, self-satisfied, symbolic machine:

> All he sees is immediately made
> an emblem, a symbol, a fable,
> the visible world a mere preaching aid,
> even the food mother lays on the table.

(GG 29)

The speaker attempts to oppose that process ('I'm so weary of all metaphorers') but does so, after all, not precisely by abandoning metaphor, but by reclaiming the material object as a metaphor *for* its very materiality – and the sensual enjoyment of that materiality – rather than as an emblem of spatial and temporal transcendence:

> *He* could take a pomegranate,
> best subjected to kisses and suction,
> and somehow make it stand for the planet
> destined for fiery destruction.

The project is problematic, though, in the terms of its own argument, if the sensuous celebration of food and sex that this poem stands by is, in the end, on the page, another 'mere preaching aid', another closed and complete system of symbols. The frustration we might feel within such systems, the howl that, I would suggest, is not quite heard within the jigsawed metaphors of *Black Daisies*, is heard – if we listen for it – in the last verse of this poem:

> The stars won't fall
> nor will the fig.
> Our hearts are so full
> as we fuck, fuck.

There are harsh rhythms and broken rhymes there, as if the materiality that Harrison seeks to work a grain against his own metaphorizing imagination (against the Gorgon in the head that reduces people to objects in a plan) is verse itself, and action: as if, somehow, these could be merely themselves. But there is desperation there too to be heard behind the celebration.

The full range of these themes is put onto the stage in *Trackers*. Here, for example, in the figure of Apollo, is the Gorgon-artist, the terrorism of ideological coercion, as the god appears – first as spectre – to demand his own embodiment and the reconstruction of the text (a very material text) in which he violently reclaims his authority to make beautiful music; before abandoning the text, the stage, this play, to return to the transcendental signifier ('I'm off to [. . .] my very own temple just down the road', in the Delphi version, *TO* 56). He leaves what remains of the text, the satyrs born out of the papyri, his aides, to history, to destitution, to dispossession and fighting amongst themselves. Here, too, we have a staging of the archaeology of scholarship, literally in Grenfell's and Hunt's bringing to light the Oxyrhyncus papyri, but also magically in the tracking itself, the reading of droppings, the sniffing for clues that approaches, in the syntax of the present, the grammar of what was already there, repressed in forgetting and ignorance. A psychoanalysis perhaps of cultural production and consumption, though Harrison himself would rather use the analogy of the detective of popular fiction (Grenfell and Hunt were 'the Holmes and Watson of Oxford papyrology') than that of the Freudian analyst (p. xv). What impresses most about the play, however, is its staging of 'the unique occasion [. . .] the secret of the glory of the continuously passing present of performance'.[13]

64

This is made obvious, of course, in Harrison's rewriting of the text for each particular performance context; but the theme itself, of how 'the inexorability of transience' is heard to speak, and speak boldly, out of and against the text, the drama, the poem, that stares its own subjects back into silence, is realized too in the basic narrative structure that is common to both published versions of the play.

If my own tortured syntax here makes the drama sound ineloquent, unapproachable; the reader should be assured that Harrison's play is anything but, and perhaps a brief summary is called for. But first some background:

> Until the end of the last century our knowledge of ancient texts depended almost entirely on copies made during the Middle Ages [...]. But a remarkable change was brought about when the archaeologists working in Egypt brought to light quantities of ancient books, often generically known as papyri even though a substantial minority of them are in fact written on parchment. The biggest finds were made at Oxyrhyncus in the Fayum by B. P. Grenfell and A. S. Hunt. For the first time scholars could consult a mass of ancient books, which are on average about a thousand years older than the textual witnesses they had to rely on before. [...] The survival of the papyri was made possible because in the villages refuse, including waste paper, was thrown on to huge rubbish dumps, which rose high enough to make their contents immune from any effects of moisture [...].[14]

Among the finds were a few hundred lines of Sophocles' satyr play *Ichneutae* ('The Trackers'), a significant find because previously the only substantial example of this form that has survived had been Euripides' *Cyclops*. Harrison's own play stages the finding of the papyri by Grenfell and Hunt (with plenty of Harrisonian wordplay on the relation between deathless literature and compost), and stages also a reconstruction of Sophocles' fragmented text – which is itself a story about following clues, putting together a puzzle: the result of said puzzle being the discovery of the lyre, Apollo's appropriation of the instrument (and the subsequent institutionalizing of quality art), and the betrayal of the trackers themselves, the foot-soldiers, the proles, the many, the satyrs. The main event of the play, for me, is an effect of temporality. The satyrs are literally born out of the ancient text, the papyri, that dresses the stage, but having been born into bodies they have entered the contemporaneous: they are, in each of their particular bodies, subject to 'the inexorability of transience – to forgetting, to erasure, to death. They occupy, then, the frustration, the howl of the subject who is subjectified by literature's alienating symbolic systems. They become, as in the London version, versions of the vandalizing yob described in *v*., the poet's alter ego who attempts to deface, with blunt inarticulacy, the articulate machine (the poem, the memorializing stone) that speaks his dispossession for him:

> But the young ones, they're bitter. They're not like me,
> they deface and destroy all papyri they see.
> They gash 'em, graffiti 'em, ay, and they'd spray
> FUCK, PISS and SHIT all over our play [...].

(p. 127, London version)

The same London version of the play ends, then, with precisely that howl – a howl on behalf of real pain, for the flayed satyr Marsyas, the original scholarship boy who was prevented from occupying poetry's lousy leasehold. But also, intelligently, that howl is ironized, it is staged as a rehearsal, it is uttered in a worn-out language. It is precisely that ironic recognition of the inevitability of theatre's appropriation of suffering into a signifying practice that *occludes* that suffering, that *enables*, after all, that suffering to be heard *somewhere else*, wherever it is that art cannot touch:

> ([...] SILENUS *tenderly wraps the* PALE BOY *in his 'cloak' and leads him to the sleeping place. Then* SILENUS *gives the cloak to the* PALE BOY *and climbs the stairs to the tragic stage.)*
>
> μη μεταναστηζ... WOE! WOE! WOE!
>
> Not bad for a satyr for his first go.
>
> (A burst of Apollo music from the Royal Festival Hall wipes the pleasure off the face of SILENUS and he stares up the centre gangway as if he sees APOLLO and the flayers coming down it.
> His mouth opens in a silent scream.
> Blackout.)

(pp. 135–6)

That somewhere else, though, is under the erasure of a blackout. The blackout finds its eloquent negative in the blank white page that follows the final full colon of 'A Cold Coming', that poem where Harrison presumes, again, to 'record' the silence of the

Gorgon's victim and find words to occupy the silence.[15] The blank page reminds us that the dead said nothing, nothing to fill the tape-recorder, and that the poem was an impersonation. At last, though, we must look for eloquence – whatever its shortcomings – in neither blackouts nor blank pages but in what has been chosen to be said. That choosing to look the evidence in the face and attempting to speak on 'its' behalf – to retrieve 'it' as a 'he', a 'she' – is what distinguishes the poet from the Gorgon. I suspect that the title of the Gulf War poem 'A Cold Coming' prods us to hear an allusion to T. S. Eliot's meditations on the interchangeability of birth and death in his poem 'The Journey of the Magi'. I suggest instead, though, that we hear an allusion to Yeats's 'The Second Coming' where the poet, attempting to mediate global crisis with the mere resources of his imagination, finds himself fashioning an Apollonian Gorgon of his own, of *himself* with 'a gaze blank and pitiless as the sun'. Such a terrifying vision is not to be rejected but be coped with. Yeats copes, or attempts to ('Cast a cold eye', although that is another story). So too, though, does Harrison – by focusing his gaze, and by trying to utter words to speak the pity, to speak *for* the pity. Poetry could do worse than this, and Harrison's eloquence has addressed that point too.

Epilogue

Meanwhile, Harrison is still producing work. His writing through to the mid 1990s, especially for the theatre and television, has continued to develop those same themes and strategies – of remembrance and translation, of facing up to worst things, of speaking on behalf of the silenced – that had been established in the earlier works considered already in this book. Furthermore, these themes have been re-rehearsed without any sort of easily pacifying conclusions or closures having been established. Rather, Harrison is still insistent upon drawing paradox and even pessimism out of his materials, while at the same time offering the material of poetry itself – its ability to persist in the face of difficulty and terror – as a counterweight to that same pessimism. However, it would seem to be a mistake to read his work simplistically in terms of themes and rhetoric. The work now almost insists that it be considered in its *public* context. Unlike the self-proclaimed Airedale poet John Nicholson, the hero of the 1993 theatre piece *Poetry or Bust* (written and performed exclusively for a production at Bradford's Salt Mill), Harrison is not now 'permanently barred'.[1] In fact his work, as far as poetry goes (and he has taken it to places that it has seldom gone before) is widely disseminated, his films are televised, his theatre receives prominent large-scale production, while sustaining – along with those qualities of tricksy playfulness and erudition which Harrison has never abandoned – a certain accessibility: a fidelity to the everyday, to the vernaculars of ordinary speech and experience, to the clarity of symbols, and to political and cultural issues of widespread import. That is to say, the significance of his work is as much involved in the *ways* that it makes sense – for example to audiences who might not otherwise turn to verse for their pleasure and instruction – as it is in the particular sense it might make, as it were, in itself. Issues of accessibility, involving access to the artwork, its means of production, and the means by which it might be decoded and understood, are vital aspects of Harrison's achievement as a public poet.

For a brief example of the sort of concerns involved here we might consider the 1994 film/poem *A Maybe Day in Kazakhstan* (*SH* 19–27), which responded to the possible establishment of a liberal-capitalist 'democracy' in the former Soviet Union since 'Communism's fatal crash':

> tubas with missiles mirrored in,
> now, unregimented, can begin
> to learn a new tune for today
> and play a fanfare not for May
> but Maybe Day and that maybe
> 's the future of democracy.

The text is largely recited over film of displaced, impoverished Kazakhstanis in modern Greece – the site of democracy's ancient birth – flogging Communism's sad souvenirs at a flea market: bronze Lenin dolls, red flags and 'surplus Soviet secateurs'. This material is now junk, sustaining little more than kitsch value at this pathetic parody of the 'free market'; and while the impetus of the film/poem is future-oriented, whispering a vaguely-defined hope, of sorts, in its repeated 'Maybe', the prevailing tone is of an ironical, almost whimsical cynicism. 'The New World Order thinks we're wiser/ then every man's a merchandiser.' The theme, then, is worked out through images of a particular accessibility, that is, the availability of commodities for ready cash. This theme is exacerbated, however, by the form, structure and context of the film/poem itself. As the traders offer their wares to passers-by at the market, the camera, selecting its own items, accesses the objects as *symbolic* commodities that constitute the terms of the poet-film-maker's exchange with his audience. So, for example, in his introduction to *The Shadow of Hiroshima and other film/poems*, Peter Symes, the director of many of Harrison's earlier film/poems, can recall 'the witty use of a Trotsky doll with revolving eyes to make fun of the Soviet ideal of permanent revolution' (*SH* p. xxi). It is as if, from the viewer's point of view, the camera picks up its souvenirs at the market without having to put money down, thereby emphasizing the vulnerability of these displaced victims of history, 'this band of Greeks who get called

69

Russian'. The narrative of the piece combines with the images and with the incorporation of the Kazakhstanis' actual voices into the spoken text (they only speak one word, 'Kazakhstan', as if that place were the scene we are being shown) to underline this point, only revealing late in the film that this scene is in fact taking place in Greece and not the former Soviet Union. This twist might surprise us, drawing attention to the documentary film medium's modes of access to other people's histories and experience, perhaps encouraging us to pause as we consider how art of this sort, in organizing its images and bringing them into our living-rooms, participates in the actual displacement and appropriation of people that art might appear to set its face against.

This apparent staging of what we might call the problematic of accessibility is followed through in Harrison's most recent piece, the film/poem *The Shadow of Hiroshima*.[2] In 1995 Harrison has shown two major pieces of work, the play *The Kaisers of Carnuntum*, performed for two nights only at the Roman amphitheatre at Carnuntum outside Vienna, and *The Shadow of Hiroshima*, broadcast by Channel 4 television on the occasion of the fiftieth anniversary of the atomic bombing of the Japanese city. Both pieces are rememberings of massive historical violence – *Kaisers* recalls imperial tyranny on the spot where tyranny, in the person of the philosopher emperor Marcus Aurelius's 'bestial' son Commodus, staged its own pageant of itself in the form of the public slaughter of beasts and people nearly 2,000 years ago.[3] Both pieces too, devised for unique commemorative occasions, addressing themselves to 'pasts' of distinct distances, are designed to trouble audiences with the suggestion that the violence they remember has not, in our own time, been put to rest. *Kaisers* concludes with the resurrection of the brutal Commodus after his execution and the ritual cleansing of the arena have already taken place; *Shadow* finds the Hiroshima ghosts still uneasy, the peace doves released for the commemoration ceremony failing to find a safe way home.

Shadow sits oddly between drama and documentary forms. More than any of Harrison's previous film/poems this one follows named characters through a staged narrative. We see a young man, Mitsufuji San, tending his pigeons, playing pinball, meeting his girlfriend Sonoko at a Love Hotel, and fretting over his pigeons after their release at the next day's A-bomb commemoration ceremony. This material is already odd because we are given to presume, according to the on-location documentary conventions on show, that Mitsufuji and the other characters encountered are 'real' inhabitants of present-day Hiroshima, although there are scenes – such as that in the Love Hotel – where they appear to be *playing* themselves, like actors. There is an effect of difficulty, appropriate to the explicit occasion of the piece, in taking on board the actuality of what we are shown. So, to take an example from one of the film's smaller narrative strands, we watch Hara San, an A-bomb survivor, painting, as he does each year on 5–6 August, a view of the A-bomb dome, the shell of a building left standing after the blast as a memorial. Again, we presume that Hara himself is not a fiction, but in the closing credit sequence we see his painting properly destroyed, dissolved on screen as if by a blast. This therefore appears as a real loss, rather than an image *of* loss. The actual documenting of these people and their activities, the camera's gaze itself, touches the material, it has an effect on the world beyond the lens.

Meanwhile these scenes, and the urban landscape of contemporary Hiroshima, are viewed through the eyes and impressions of a fiction, another one of those Harrisonian presiding vantages recalled from the silenced and petrified stone:

> 'This voice comes from the shadow cast
> by Hiroshima's A-bomb blast.
> The sound you hear inside this case
> is of a man who fans the face
> he used to have before the flash
> turned face and body into ash.
> I am the nameless fanning man
> you may address as Shadow San.'

Shadow San's shadow is cast upon various of the dramatized scenes; the camera stands in for his point of view (which is also of course our point of view); and Harrison's spoken text – as in the brief passage quoted above – slips between third-person commentary and an imagined first-person testimony. There is, then, an explicit tension between the real thing (be that the mere documentary material on Hiroshima 1995 or that 'worst thing', the bomb blast back in Hiroshima 1945) and the imaginative modes by means of which that thing is being accessed.

This tension is vital, it seems to me, to the extent that it trips up the imagination's appropriation of horrors into a comfortably *redemptive* fiction; and the challenging of this fiction is effected by the sense of appropriation that runs throughout the piece. For example, there is what appears to be a felt contempt for the economic pervasion of multinationals like Coca Cola in *Shadow*, but at the same time there is an appropriation and re-offering of their brand logos (visible all over the city) as symbolic capital that enables Shadow San/Harrison to make arguments about remembrance and erasure economically, as it were. Similarly, there is a peculiar sense of appropriation in the incorporation of Shadow San himself as a narrating vantage in the film. We might look at precedents for the use of guiding ghosts, perhaps in the Japanese Noh drama tradition, or in Western examples such as Dante's *Divine Comedy* (the poet Virgil who guides Dante through Hell, Purgatory and Paradise) or Shakespeare's *Hamlet* (the ghost of Hamlet's father who informs his son of the causes of the present state of affairs in Denmark). In all these cases, however, the relationship between the ghost and the living protagonist is a personal one, a case of a peculiar privilege that almost amounts to a right. Both Dante and Hamlet are elected to be given the ghost's message. Harrison's narrator-persona does not have this same privilege, quite. In 'A Cold Coming' the ghost of the dead Iraqi soldier was called out of a news agency photograph, and Harrison's poet took on something of the impersonal role of foreign correspondent, consuming material with a portable tape-recorder. In *Shadow* the ghost is given to rise from a public monument, and there is no particular relationship between ghost and poet. The poet just assumes access, of a sort; and, in fact, in Harrison's version of the form there is an odd twist, because here it is the contemporary arriviste who takes the role of the tour guide. The ghost is re-introduced to a home they barely recognize since its obliteration and rebuilding, by a foreigner who ventriloquizes the ghost's 'translation' of what is shown.

In short, the film/poem exploits a tension between the externality of the camera and the internality, so to speak, of the poet's speaking voice: playing between the 'objective' reconstructions of documentary and the 'subjective' reconstructions of poetry in such a way as to unsettle the assumptions of such a simple binarism. So often in this film the camera is at thresholds, directed at doors, at entrance signs, at public notices, at printed programmes; or at objects such as unfamiliar brands of cigarettes; or at the façades of public buildings; or at rituals which it makes no attempt to fully explain, which it cannot claim to fully understand – the Shinto ceremony, baseball training, the preparation of sushi, the bomb commemoration ceremony itself. Or else the camera gazes at people, Japanese people, going about private business, speaking a language that is foreign to most of the viewing audience. Harrison's voice, meanwhile, measured, persistent, is layered over all this – but speaking at the same time from both without and within the scene, narrating it, thinking its thoughts, channelling our access to these images. At the same time, there is only so far he can go. He is after all, in actual fact, recording his text back home in the studio. As in *Maybe Day* Harrison's voice is disembodied, he does not appear on the screen, although his text is as personalized, as much his own and no one else's, as ever. This sets up the convention that he can appear, as the tourist documenter, to go wherever he chooses, he can peer into intimacies even if, as a non-Japanese, or like the dead Shadow San himself, he cannot *be* intimate with the scenes he views.

If we read, as I believe Harrison's work here gives us leave to do, the voice as an interlocutor with the images, rather than as a transparent commentary upon what we see on the screen, then accessibility is compromised by being so blatantly staged. The valuable effect of this compromise is, as I have suggested, to question the facility of a fully *redemptive* fiction. Harrison is explicit enough on this score. In the fiction that he has produced Shadow San only returns as an insubstantiality, and then only for a day; even his actual shadow is already fading (and thereby remembrance itself is under siege – just as the ageing Hiroshima survivors themselves are fewer each year). Similarly there is hardly any soft-pedalling on the bitterness and regret for being absent from the world of the living. Furthermore, the text's conclusion offers a direct challenge to the sentimental assumption of a redemptive fantasy:

> These symbolic doves that flew
> in '91 or '92
> in '93 or 4 survive
> by fighting those from '95...
> Pigeon/Peace-doves brawl and fight.

73

Is the world at peace tonight?
Or are we all like Shadow San
facing inferno with a fan?

This challenge, both dogmatic and formalistic, to the takeaway satisfaction of a symbol, seems, in the present context, to establish a proper relationship between the living and the betrayed dead. It is proper enough that the living should put out peace-doves and eloquent images into the air of the present, but it is proper also, if all this *is* a question of the relationship between the living and the dead, between those who have access to the world and those who do not, that consideration be given to the substance of an image and the technology of its dissemination. Sometimes an image is too much, sometimes an image is not enough. Harrison, at his best, weighs those options against each other.

Notes

CHAPTER 1: LANDSCAPE, LEXICON AND LOVE

1. All quotations will be from the second British edition of *Selected Poems*. There are discrepancies between this and the second American selection (*V. and Other Poems*) which includes some poems collected in *The Gaze of the Gorgon*. Although *Selected Poems* silently omits certain early verses – most notably the whole of *Earthworks* and a few poems of *The Loiners* – for the purpose of this brief study I shall restrict my comments to considerations of lyrics in this volume. *Selected Poems* (abbreviated as *SP* in my references) is not to be confused with the 1995 publication *Permanently Bard: Selected Poetry*, which is a genuine 'selected', as it were.
2. My modifying phrases 'more or less' and 'as good as' as applied to the iambic pattern of the metre and the fondness of recollection are there to suggest an extent to which the regularity of the iambic pattern is disturbed by an unsettled scepticism (a pessimism of the intellect) in the process of recall. Luke Spencer elaborates on this same point (Spencer, p. 17).
3. Biographical details will be variously lifted throughout from Rosemary Burton's essay 'Tony Harrison: An Introduction', in Neil Astley, *Tony Harrison*, pp. 14–31; and from the Chronology in Luke Spencer, *The Poetry of Tony Harrison*, pp. xiii–xv.
4. We should add here that Peru is not 'anywhere'. The particular place recalls a particular (and particularly brutal) history of imperialistic appropriation and exploitation. As Spencer reminds us, remembering John Donne's 'my America! my new-found land', this exploitation is echoed in the sexual scene and the 'discovery' that, at one level, is to stand as a counter to such violent histories. See *The Poetry of Tony Harrison*, pp. 36–7.

CHAPTER 2: TRANSLATIONS

1. Romy Heylen, *Translation, Poetics, and the Stage: Six French 'Hamlets'*

(London: Routledge, 1993), pp. 23, 24.

2. Readers interested in these issues are referred to the whole of Walter Benjamin's fascinating essay 'The Task of the Translator', in Benjamin, *Illuminations*, ed. Hannah Arendt, trans. Harry Zohn (Glasgow: Fontana/Collins, 1973), pp. 60–82. For more recent comments on the ethics of translation as reading and 'translation in general' in a particularly postcolonial context see Gayatri Chakravorty Spivak, 'The Politics of Translation', in her *Outside in the Teaching Machine* (London: Routledge, 1993), pp. 179–200.

3. Heylen, p. 20.

4. The misogynistic undertone to my word 'bitchy' is intentional. Harrison stages a gendered resentment in both the Palladas and Martial sequences. Spencer has elaborated on this politics, and goes so far as to implicate Harrison himself in the attitudes of what would then be, to a certain extent, personae of the poet that translates (Spencer, ch. 3). Although I agree with the direction of Spencer's remarks I would want to emphasise the particular job of the *dramatist* so as to point out a more difficult complicity between a writer and his 'characters' (in both the orthographic and the theatrical senses of that word). I elaborate on this point in the last chapter of the present work.

5. By all accounts the trilogy comprised versions of the Aristophanes play, Euripides' *The Trojan Women*, and an original play, *Maxims*. The Aristophanes piece has been published under the title *The Common Chorus*, and *Maxims* has been reworked, performed and published as *Square Rounds*. The latter play's origin in the trilogy is recalled by its general anti-war sentiment and its largely all-female cast.

6. I am paraphrasing Harrison's comments in Astley's *Tony Harrison*, pp. 84–7. At a later date Harrison writes of *Aikin Mata* as having been 'responsive to the tensions that later erupted into a devastating civil war' (*CC*, p. xii).

7. I am quoting from the selection of Harrison's correspondence with the trilogy's director Peter Hall (Astley, pp. 275–80).

8. Roland Barthes, *Camera Lucida: Reflections on Photography*, trans. Richard Howard (London: Vintage, 1993), pp. 116–7. The referencing of Barthes is not gratuitous. Readers of Harrison poems such as 'Background Material' or 'Sonnets for August 1945' are unreservedly referred to the whole of Barthes's book.

9. *Aeschylus 1: Oresteia*, trans. Richard Lattimore (Chicago: University of Chicago Press, 1953), pp. 64–5.

10. Louis MacNiece, *Selected Poems*, ed. W. H. Auden (London: Faber and Faber, 1964), p. 159.

11. 'The Mysteries: T. W.'s Revenge' (Astley, pp. 316–23). O'Donoghue points readers to scholarly editions of all the cycles published by the Early English Text Society (Oxford University Press), and recom-

mends P. Happé's 'useful composite cycle', *English Mystery Plays* (Harmondsworth: Penguin, 1975).

12. 'Introduction', *The Faber Book of Vernacular Verse*, ed. Tom Paulin (London: Faber and Faber, 1990), pp. xxi–xxii.

13. *The Wakefield Pageants in the Towneley Cycle*, ed. A. C. Cawley (Manchester: Manchester University Press, 1958), pp. 48–9.

14. Spencer makes a much more detailed sampling than I have room for here of the variety of effects in *The Mysteries*, (pp. 51–5).

CHAPTER 3: REMEMBRANCE

1. The poem is printed in Astley's *Tony Harrison*, pp. 496–503, and *The Gaze of the Gorgon*, pp. 38–45.

2. Aeschylus, *Prometheus Bound, The Suppliants, Seven Against Thebes, The Persians*, trans. Philip Vellacott (Harmondsworth: Penguin, 1961), p. 34.

3. Tom Paulin, *Seize the Fire: A Version of Aeschylus's 'Prometheus Unbound'* (London: Faber, 1990), p. 31.

4. Spencer is good on the role of the 'mother' in Harrison's work. As in my own comments, he is not talking about Harrison's *actual* mother but of the mother as a structuring principle to the extent to which she appears (or does not appear) in the published work. Spencer makes the interesting point that the mother is at times given a 'puritan' role – something akin perhaps to the role I assign to the remembered 'community' in my first chapter. See *The Poetry of Tony Harrison*, pp. 39, 88–9.

5. Ezra Pound, *The Cantos of Ezra Pound* (London: Faber, 1975), p. 796.

6. The poem has not yet been incorporated into the *School* sequence, and maybe it will not be, but its form and its concerns make it one of the most recent instances of much that is typical about the sequence.

7. For an elaboration of these points see Rick Rylance's essay, 'On Not Being Milton', (Astley, pp. 114–28).

8. According to Harrison this rhetorical excess is only apparent. Phone cables really did melt in Leeds. See his preface to *Trackers* (*TO*, pp. vii–viii).

9. He does, in plays like *The Common Chorus* and *Square Rounds*, seem to sympathize with a unilateral pacificism, but even there the pacifist appeal is shown not to be fully effective, politically, as yet.

10. J. M. Barrie, *The Plays of J. M. Barrie* (London: Hodder and Stoughton, 1929), p. 42.

11. Spencer seems to be saying something similar: 'the great achievement of the poem is finally in allowing its own dialectic – its commitment to the 'versus' principle, no matter where it leads – to provide the means by which its attempted closure can be

deconstructed' (Spencer, p. 99).

CHAPTER 4: THE POET AND THE GORGON

1. For the reference to Hesiod I am indebted to Anthony Kubiak's *Stages of Terror: Terrorism, Ideology, and Coercion as Theatre History* (Bloomington, Indiana University Press, 1991), in particular the opening chapter. Much of what follows is informed by Kubiak's argument. The Phobos image in Hesiod appears in the *Theogony* (ll. 934–8) and *The Shield of Herakles* (ll. 143–7).
2. The text is published in Astley's *Tony Harrison*, pp. 395–406; and *The Shadow of Hiroshima and other film/poems*, pp. 51–64, with additional verses that were previously suppressed.
3. *The Oxford Book of Modern Verse*, ed. W. B. Yeats (Oxford: Clarendon Press, 1936).
4. Hovering behind these comments is Jacques Derrida's Heideggerian discussion of how one might speak of 'death' in his *Aporias: Dying – awaiting (one another at) the 'limits of truth'*, trans. Thomas Dutoit (Stanford University Press, 1993). There might also be a pertinent space for Derrida in the previous chapter of the present work, in particular his meditations on mourning, Hamlet and the spectre of the father, and the political obligations attendant upon conjuring certain Marxisms in his *Specters of Marx: The State of the Debt, the Work of Mourning, and the New International*, trans. Peggy Kamuf (London: Routledge, 1995).
5. I quote from my own unpublished translation of Müller's *Shagged Shore / Medeamaterial / Landscape with Argonauts* which was performed in 1989. For the whole play readers are referred to Carl Weber's perfectly adequate version in *Hamletmachine and Other Texts for the Stage*, ed. and trans. Weber (New York: PAJ, 1984); or Marc von Henning's in *Theatremachine*, ed. von Henning (London: Faber, 1995). Harrison, of course, has written his own version in 1985 of Medea in *Medea: A Sex-War Opera* (TW, pp. 365–448).
6. Tony Harrison, *The Common Chorus* (London: Faber, 1992), pp. x–xi. Harrison quotes the Greek. I have inserted Richard Lattimore's translation from *The Complete Greek Tragedies*, vol. 3, *Euripides* (Chicago: University of Chicago Press, 1959), p. 657. The extract from Hecuba's speech occupies lines 1242–45.
7. The address, 'Facing Up to the Muses', is printed in Astley's *Tony Harrison*, pp. 429–54. Harrison was president of the Classical Association in 1987–8.
8. Astley, p. 447.
9. Hesiod, *Works and Days*, ll. 180–1, in *Hesiod The Homeric Hymns and*

Homerica, trans. Hugh G. Evelyn-White, Loeb Classical Library (London: Heinemann, 1977), pp. 16–17.

10. Tony Harrison, *Black Daisies for the Bride* (London: Faber, 1993), p. 26.
11. BBC2, *The Late Show*, which included an interview conducted between Harrison and Michael Ignatieff.
12. The reviews of *Square Rounds* can be read in *Theatre Record* (23 September – 6 October, 1992), 1163–9. The second (1989) edition of *v.* prints a selection of documents out of the controversy over the Channel 4 broadcast of Richard Eyre's film of the poem.
13. *CC*, p. v.
14. D. Reynolds and N. G. Wilson, *Scribes and Scholars: A Guide to the Transmission of Greek and Latin Literature*, 2nd edn (Oxford: Clarendon, 1974), pp. 177–8.
15. A word from another poet-dramatist might be appropriate here: 'The dead are only dead in so far as they continue to exist in the heart of the survivor. And pity for what has been suffered is a more cruel and precise expression for that suffering than the conscious estimate of the sufferer, who is spared at least one despair – the despair of the spectator' (Samuel Beckett, *Proust* (New York: Grove, no date), p. 29; quoted in Herbert Blau, *The Eye of Prey: Subversions of the Postmodern*, Bloomington: Indiana University Press, 1987), p. 94.

EPILOGUE

1. An excerpt from *Poetry or Bust* is printed in Carol Rutter's punningly titled *Tony Harrison, Permanently Bard: Selected Poetry* (Newcastle upon Tyne: Bloodaxe, 1995).
2. *SH*, pp. 1–17. This is the first film/poem to receive the credit 'Written and directed by Tony Harrison'. Although of course the film-making process is still one of close collaboration – the contribution of the composer Richard Blackford is particularly significant here – the direction credit allows us to consider the organization of images as an author's strategy, in much the same way as we might consider, say, the ordering of poems in a book.
3. An excerpt from *The Kaisers of Carnuntum* was printed in the *Guardian*, 27 May 1995, although the play-text as a whole is as yet unpublished. Referring to this show, in the *Independent* interview, 5 August, Harrison suggests that 'In fact it might be the best thing I've ever done. And I don't usually think that.'

Select Bibliography

WORKS BY TONY HARRISON

Earthworks by T. W. Harrison (Leeds: Northern House, 1964). A nine-poem pamphlet, Harrison's first collection.

Aikin Mata (Ibadan: Oxford University Press, 1966). The adaptation, with James Simmons, of Aristophanes' *Lysistrata* in a Nigerian setting.

Newcastle is Peru (Leeds: Eagle Press, 1969; Newcastle upon Tyne: Northern House, 1974). Single-poem pamphlet.

The Loiners (London Magazine Editions, 1970). His first book-length collection.

The Misanthrope (London: Rex Collings, 1973). Version of Molière's *Le Misanthrope* for the National Theatre. Second edition (1975) included prefatory materials by Harrison, now printed in Astley's *Tony Harrison*.

Phaedra Britannica (London: Rex Collings, 1975). Version of Racine's *Phèdre* for the National Theatre. Third edition (1976) included Harrison's preface, as printed in Astley's *Tony Harrison*.

The Blue Bird (1975). Song lyrics for George Cukor's film of Maeterlink's play. Unpublished.

Palladas: Poems (London: Anvil Press Poetry, 1975; 1984). Translations from the fourth-century Alexandrian poet Palladas.

Bow Down (London: Rex Collings, 1977). Devised by Harrison with the National Theatre, to a score by Harrison Birtwistle.

The Passion (London: Rex Collings, 1977). First version of the National Theatre adaptation of 14 plays from the York Mystery Cycle.

The Bartered Bride (New York: G. Schirmer, 1978). Harrison's version of Karel Sabina's original Czech libretto for Smetana's opera, performed by the New York Metropolitan Opera.

From 'The School of Eloquence' and Other Poems (London: Rex Collings, 1978). Harrison's second book-length collection.

Continuous: 50 Sonnets from 'The School of Eloquence, (London: Rex Collings, 1981). Expands the sequence from 18 to 50 poems.

Arctic Paradise (1981). Verse commentary for Andree Molyneux's film for

BBC2's *World About Us* series. Published in Astley's *Tony Harrison*, pp. 377–81.

The Oresteia (London: Rex Collings, 1981). Harrison's version of Aeschylus's trilogy for the National Theatre, later shown on Channel Four on 9 October 1983.

A Kumquat for John Keats (Newcastle upon Tyne: Bloodaxe, 1981). Single-poem pamphlet.

U. S. Martial (Newcastle upon Tyne: Bloodaxe Books, 1981). Translations from the Roman poet Martial.

Yan Tan Tethera (1983). 'A Mechanical Pastoral' with text by Harrison and music by Harrison Birtwistle, commissioned by BBC, performed by the Opera Factory with the London Sinfonietta at the Queen Elizabeth Hall on 5 August 1986, and shown on Channel Four on 19 April 1987.

The Big H (1984). Music drama produced by Andree Molyneux, music by Dominic Muldowney, performed on BBC2 on 26 December 1984.

Selected Poems (Harmondsworth: Penguin, 1984). American edition published by Random House in 1987, Harrisons first book to be published in America. Expands *The School of Eloquence* to 67 sonnets.

The Mysteries (London: Faber, 1985). Revised by Harrison with the National Theatre; shown on Channel Four in December–January 1985–6.

Medea: a sex-war opera (1985). Commissioned by the New York Metropolitan Opera for music by Jacob Druckman. The music was not produced and the opera was not performed.

v. (Newcastle upon Tyne: Bloodaxe, 1985). Contains 14 photographs by Graham Sykes. Richard Eyre's film of the poem was shown on Channel 4 on 4 November 1987.

The Fire-Gap (Newcastle-upon Tyne: Bloodaxe, 1985). Single-poem poster-book.

Theatre Works, 1973–1985 (Harmondsworth: Penguin, 1986). Identical in content to *Dramatic Verse 1973–1985* (Newcastle upon Tyne: Bloodaxe, 1985), containing the complete texts of *The Misanthrope*, *Phaedra Britannica*, *Bow Down*, *The Bartered Bride*, *The Oresteia*, *Yan Tan Tethera*, *The Big H*, and *Medea: a sex-war opera*.

Loving Memory (1987), four film/poems directed by Peter Symes for BBC Bristol, shown in July–August 1987. Text published in *The Shadow of Hiroshima and other film/poems*.

Selected Poems (Harmondsworth: Penguin, 1987), 2nd edition. Expands *The School of Eloquence* to 78 sonnets. Includes *v.* and adds 'The Fire-Gap', 'The Heartless Art' and 'Following Pine' to the first edition.

v.: new edition, with press articles (Newcastle upon Tyne: Bloodaxe, 1989), 2nd edition. Includes 7 photographs by Graham Sykes as well as an extensive selection of documents surrounding the controversy over Channel 4's film of the poem.

The Blasphemers' Banquet (1989). Film/poem directed by Peter Symes and

81

shown on BBC1 on 31 July 1989. Published in Astley *Tony Harrison* pp. 395–406, and *The Shadow of Hiroshima and other film/poems.*

V. and Other Poems (New York: Farrar Straus Giroux, 1990). Harrison's second American book of poems, includes pieces that appear in *The Gaze of the Gorgon.*

The Trackers of Oxyrhyncus (London: Faber, 1990). Contains texts for both productions of the play at Delphi and the National Theatre.

A Cold Coming: Gulf War Poems (Newcastle upon Tyne: Bloodaxe, 1991). Two poems collected in *The Gaze of the Gorgon.*

The Common Chorus (London: Faber, 1992). Harrison's unperformed Greenham-Common-based version of *Lysistrata.*

The Gaze of the Gorgon (1992). Film/poem directed by Peter Symes, shown on BBC2 on 3 October 1992. Text published in *The Gaze of the Gorgon* and *The Shadow of Hiroshima and other film/poems.*

Square Rounds (London: Faber, 1992). Text for National Theatre production.

The Gaze of the Gorgon (Newcastle upon Tyne: Bloodaxe, 1992). Harrison's latest collection of poems.

Black Daisies for the Bride (London: Faber, 1993). Film/poem broadcast by BBC 2 on 30 June 1993.

Poetry or Bust (1993). Play about the self-proclaimed Airedale poet John Nicholson, written and performed in September 1993 at Salt's Mill in Bradford to coincide with an exhibition of the artist David Hockney.

A Maybe Day in Kazakhstan (1994). Film/poem for Channel 4 shown in May 1994, published as Channel 4 booklet and in *The Shadow of Hiroshima and other film/poems.*

The Kaisers of Carnuntum (1995). Performed at the Roman amphitheatre at Carnuntum outside Vienna on 2 and 3 June 1995.

The Shadow of Hiroshima (1995). Film/poem for Channel 4's *Witness* series, written and directed by Harrison, to commemorate the fiftieth anniversary of the Hiroshima bomb. Broadcast 6 August 1995.

The Shadow of Hiroshima and other film/poems (London: Faber, 1995). Includes the texts of *The Shadow of Hiroshima, A Maybe Day in Kazakhstan, The Gaze of the Gorgon, The Blasphemers' Banquet,* and *Loving Memory.* With an introduction by Peter Symes, the director of many of Harrison's earlier film/poems.

Permanently Bard: Selected Poetry, ed. Carol Rutter (Newcastle upon Tyne: Bloodaxe, 1995). Includes a passage from *Poetry or Bust.*

BIBLIOGRAPHIES

Astley, Neil (ed.), *Tony Harrison: Bloodaxe Critical Anthologies 1* (Newcastle upon Tyne: Bloodaxe, 1991).

Kaiser, John R, *Tony Harrison: A Bibliography 1957–1987* (Mansell, 1989). A full bibliography of primary and secondary sources.

CRITICAL WORKS

Astley, Neil, (ed.), *Tony Harrison: Bloodaxe Critical Anthologies 1* (Newcastle upon Tyne: Bloodaxe, 1991). An enormous selection of the extant critical material on Harrison, it also includes Harrison texts which are either unprinted elsewhere or now hard to get hold of. Includes an autobiographical statement, interviews, prefaces to the plays, essays, correspondence, and the texts for the films *Arctic Paradise* and *The Blasphemers' Banquet.*

Geyer-Ryan, Helga, 'Heteroglossia in the Poetry of Bertolt Brecht and Tony Harrison', in Willie van Peer (ed.), *The Taming of the Text: Explorations in Language, Literature and Culture* (London: Routledge, 1988), pp. 193–221.

McAuley, Gay, 'Body, Space and Language: The Actor's Work on/with Text', in *Kodikas/Code/Ars Semeiotica*, vol. 12, nos. 1–2 (January–June 1989), 57–70.

Morgan, David, 'The Brilliant Obviousness of Verse', in *Drama*, no. 174 (1989), 12–13.

Rylance, Rick, 'Tony Harrison's Languages', in Antony Easthope and John Thompson (eds.), *Contemporary Poetry Meets Modern Theory* (Toronto: University of Toronto Press, 1991), pp. 53–67.

Spencer, Luke, *The Poetry of Tony Harrison* (Hemel Hempstead: Harvester Wheatsheaf, 1994). The first book-length study of Harrison's work.

Wood, Michael, 'Classics and the Scarecrow', in *Parnassus: Poetry in Review*, vol. 14, no. 2 (1988), 324–39.

Woodcock, Bruce, 'Classical Vandalism: Tony Harrison's Invective', in *Critical Quarterly*, vol. 32, no. 2 (Summer 1990), 50–65.

Young, Alan, 'Weeds and White Roses: The Poetry of Tony Harrison', in *Critical Quarterly*, vol. 26 (Spring–Summer 1984), 157–63.

Index

84